THE GRATITUDE CURVE

Using the lessons of chronic illness
to reach personal empowerment

By Gregg Kirk

©2018 By Gregg Kirk

All rights reserved. No part of this book may be reproduced in any manner without the express written consent of the author, except in the case of brief excerpts in critical reviews or articles. All inquiries should be addressed to Gregg Kirk, 115 Ward St., Norwalk, CT 06851.

ISBN-13:

978-1717166289

ISBN-10:

1717166288

The scanning, uploading and distribution of this book via the Internet or via any other means without the permission of the author is illegal and punishable by law. Please purchase only authorized electronic editions, and do not participate in or encourage electronic piracy of copyrighted materials. Your support of the author's rights is appreciated.

> "And if you gaze for long into an abyss,
> the abyss gazes also into you."
>
> — *Friedrich Nietzsche*

This is not a story of how one patient conquered chronic illness.

It's a story of how that patient listened to what the illness had to teach him.

.

CONTENTS:

	Introduction:	Pg. 1
Chapter 1:	A Clean Slate	Pg. 5
Chapter 2:	The Shape of Things to Come	Pg. 9
Chapter 3:	Healing Touch	Pg. 16
Chapter 4:	A State That Starts With a "C"	Pg. 24
Chapter 5:	Under Pressure	Pg. 30
Chapter 6:	Mystery Illness	Pg. 42
Chapter 7:	The Battle Begins	Pg. 47
Chapter 8:	Stage Two of the Battle	Pg. 57
Chapter 9:	Everything Changes	Pg. 62
Chapter 10:	New Gifts	Pg. 71
Chapter 11:	Things Shift	Pg. 89
Chapter 12:	Using the Gifts	Pg. 101
Chapter 13:	Another Shift	Pg. 110
Chapter 14:	Blast from the Past	Pg. 116
Chapter 15:	Healing Miracles	Pg. 121
Chapter 16:	Holding Current	Pg. 138
Chapter 17:	Sacred Waterfall	Pg. 146
Chapter 18:	More Healing	Pg. 151
Chapter 19:	The Land of Heavy Energy	Pg. 159

Chapter 20:	Return to Brazil	Pg. 169
Chapter 21:	Farewell to Brazil	Pg. 177
Chapter 22:	Returning Home	Pg. 185
Chapter 23:	Ticked Off	Pg. 191
Chapter 24:	Lyme Patience	Pg. 196
Chapter 25:	Deeper Information	Pg. 199
Chapter 26:	Healing in America	Pg. 205
Chapter 27:	Breaking Open	Pg. 212
Chapter 28:	The Six Stages of Healing Chronic Lyme	Pg. 219
Chapter 29:	Making Sense of it All	Pg. 227
Chapter 30:	The Gratitude Curve	Pg. 233
	Resources:	Pg. 238

ACKNOWLEDGMENTS

I would like to thank all of the people who helped make the writing and publishing of this book possible:

Special thanks to my family (especially Tracey, Carly, Myrna & Allen Kirk and Ginger Power) and our friends who were supportive during the dark days of the struggle.

Eternal thanks to João Teixeira de Faria & the generous people at the Casa de Dom Inácio de Loyola including Heather Cumming, Monica Evon, Laura Gwen and Joann Wolff.

Big thanks to Donya Wicken, her friend Ben, Tessa St. John Hughes, Steve Johnson, Bill Peerman and Aldo & Linda Esposito.

Extra thanks to Wendy Rose Williams, Catherine Ann Clemmet, Greg Marcel & Lorraine Daley Marcel, Shawn Savage & Eva Baker Savage, Justin Ram Das, Jennifer Vanderslice and Tali Tarone,

Special thanks to my friends and collaborators in the Lyme community including Lauren Lovejoy, Paula Jackson Jones, Jennifer Reid, Karen Gaudian, Michele Cloutier Miller, Stephanie at Recycle for Lyme, Katina Makris, Melissa Bell, Zina Ruben, Rev. Suzanne Cameron Stover, Jennifer Goodwin, Les Stroud, Karen Durm, Alisa Turner, Natalie London, Sandi Bohle, Mara Williams, Tim Eaton & Nutramedix, Dr. Lee Cowden and Melissa Cox.

And thanks to test readers Lyn "Tigg" Boyce, Lynnette Blaney, Donya Wicken, Wendy Rose Williams, Jennifer Vanderslice, Chris Kirk, Jeff Kirk, Jenni Bearden, Lauren Lovejoy and Tracey Kirk.

INTRODUCTION:

By GREGG KIRK
February 12, 2007, Norwalk, CT

I promised myself I would wait until I hit rock bottom before I began writing anything down about what I've been going through, and I think the last five days have provided me with that opportunity.

For more than four years I've been struggling with Lyme disease and a secondary tick-borne illness called *bartonella*. Because it took a team of doctors more than two years to diagnose me, the infection had plenty of time to set in, and as is the case with both bacterias, this makes it all the harder to treat.

I won't go into details at this point about my misdiagnosis, diagnosis, several failed attempts at treatment and trouble with insurance coverage; but suffice it to say that once I began taking antibiotics more than two years ago, my symptoms of fatigue, brain fog, depression, joint pain, and malaise were all amplified. Since then I haven't lived a single day that wasn't somehow impacted by the disease.

I recognized that fact yesterday, actually when I came to the realization that several days had passed without me feeling anything resembling a single moment of pleasure. Instead, I endured solid, non-stop physical and mental pain and felt several times during this period the need to escape my body. I say this not to be melodramatic; it's simply the reality of it.

I'm not suicidal, and I do realize there are riches around me for which I am grateful, but it's amazing how sickness can twist your perspective. It can close out the rest of the world and reduce your sphere of perception to the size of a pinhead.

The thought that kept running through my mind was something I had heard someone utter on a radio show recently — "God tests the ones he loves the most." That thought has been my talisman, because before I got sick, I felt the beauty of life and even felt blessed by god. Once those things were diminished because of sickness, I wanted to leave this world, but I was suddenly shown a different and magical view that changed everything… and then I got even sicker.

These have been dark days. Not only have I been enduring intense neurological and physical Lyme symptoms and am currently on intravenous meds, I happened to catch a particularly virulent flu from my daughter that flattened me with a deep lung and upper-respiratory infection. I was already achy, foggy, and feeling sick from the Lyme, but I never knew the agony of a serious chronic illness until I spent five straight days on my back with a fever on top of it all. My quality of life was reduced to blurry wakeful hours of being acutely aware of muscle spasms, body aches, and chills. I couldn't even enjoy a simple pleasure like the taste of food. Not only did I have no appetite, nothing tasted good to me. When I say I had no pleasure at all, I'm breaking it down to that level. Nothing enjoyable happened to me for five straight days, and instead, I experienced some of the most intense and lengthy pain of my life.

To make things a little more interesting, the regular nurse who comes to clean my PICC (peripherally inserted central catheter) dressing every Saturday had been M.I.A. for the last two weeks. This week my doctor sent a semi-retired substitute who obviously hadn't been practicing medicine for a while. This woman managed to stretch the part of my line that extends from my arm, and she punctured it while trying to change the dressing. Now I couldn't infuse my meds anymore, and I was told I needed to have the line re-installed. That was the last thing I wanted to hear. Installing a PICC line is no day at the beach. It involves poking a hole in a large vein on the inside of your elbow, running a wire lead all the way up to your heart and then threading a small plastic tube through this area. In August of 2005, I experienced a botched PICC installation where I almost died on the operating table and later that night the line jabbed into the atrium of my heart, causing strong palpitations for several months. I had the worst feelings of claustrophobia and wanted to rip the line out myself.

So, when I heard there were ways to repair PICC lines, I was hanging my hopes on that idea when I went to Norwalk Hospital on the ensuing Monday. I should've known something was up when the staff was actually waiting for me there. I didn't have to wait a second. I filled out my waiver forms and the nurse immediately received me and told me I'd be getting my line re-installed that day. I asked her about PICC repair.

"There's no such thing," she said. "Once it's broken, you need to put in a new one."

The worst was about to happen; I was about to have my third PICC installation in two years. I lay down on the table in resignation as they injected the anesthetic in my arm and moved the X-ray machines in place over my chest to monitor the line thread through to its destination... in my full view.

I have felt compelled to tell my story and begin the writing of it not knowing if there will be a happy ending. But even as I struggle through these days, I'm not without hope. I may be reeling physically and mentally, but spiritually I'm still intact. Why? Because of a set of circumstances that occurred about a year ago, I know that I will be fine. I know there are forces beyond my understanding that are not only driving the cause of my pain but the undoing of it as well. I have been a part of some minor miracles and now know that they are as commonplace as drawing a breath. The potential for miracles and great power is within us all and that shouldn't be seen as something to fear, ridicule or to ignore.

Here is my story...

CHAPTER 1:
A CLEAN SLATE

I've always held what I considered a healthy balance between belief and skepticism of the mystical, paranormal and spirituality. I think like most people, I *wanted* to believe in things like ghosts and UFOs, mainly because I thought the general idea of them was fascinating, but there was never any available proof to make me genuinely believe.

When I was 12, I read the book and saw the movie version of "Chariots of the Gods," written by Erich von Däniken. The premise that things like the Egyptian pyramids, Mayan pyramids and giant animal effigies in the Plains of Nazca couldn't have been constructed by these primitive cultures without some outside help struck a chord with me. The book made the case and put forth some compelling evidence (at least to my 12-year old mind) that aliens from other worlds had undoubtedly played a heavy role in shaping key elements in our human history.

After finishing the book, I remember going downstairs and telling my mother that I didn't believe in god anymore.

Wisely, she said, "Oh," and went back to doing whatever it was she had already been doing. Some evidence the book used from the Bible had made me think that it was the benevolent aliens we should be revering instead of the religious figures in the book who came from even shakier evidence. Had my mother put up a fight, I'm sure I would've stuck to my guns, but instead, within a few weeks I was back to believing in a more traditional version of Protestant Christianity. This view would change over time.

I was, after all, a faithful person from the time I was born. My mother told me in my later years that once when my father had taken a plane to go on a business trip, I had suggested we light a candle for his safety that night. I was barely five years old, and she admitted that the solemnity of my request and the precociousness of it had unnerved her.

And even at that age, I could distinguish between being spiritual and being religious. I was raised in a Protestant Christian family, and like most of my friends, I had reflexively hated being forced to go to Sunday school, Bible school and any other thing that had to do with organized religion. The dogma and dry approach to the message had taken all the interest out of religion for me, but somehow it had not rattled my faith in a higher being like it had for my brothers and so many of my friends who had been sentenced to Catholic schools.

I attended a vacation Bible school class two summers in a row where we were taught stories from the New Testament in workbooks that were similar to those we had in regular school. I hated it, and I remember thinking it weird that we were pasting and coloring cartoon figures of people we were supposed to be worshipping.

Toward the end of the month-long session, our teachers did something that I'll never forget. They asked those who wanted Jesus to come into their hearts to leave the room, one by one.

This separating-from-the-herd approach had the eerie feel of sending the condemned off to the concentration camp, and the first year I was too afraid to do it because of the intense delivery of the teachers: "Only those children who want Jesus to come into their hearts should follow us out the door. All others please stay in your seats and read your workbooks."

The second year, curiosity got the better of me, and I actually felt an obligation. I wanted to be closer to god and Jesus. Why shouldn't I do it?

So, I followed the teacher out of the room and into a large, walk-in closet. I can still remember the old institutional building smell of lacquered desks, tile floors and old plaster walls practically suffocating me. In the closet were two desks facing each other, and the teacher instructed me to sit at one of them. She closed the door and there we sat silently in the dark.

As my eyes adjusted to the light, I could see the teacher facing me with her hands clasped and head bowed in prayer. I half expected to see an angel of god materialize to bless my heart so that Jesus could enter.

Instead, the woman uttered some inane words about the fact that me wanting Jesus to come into my heart was the first step and that I needed to keep my faith for him to eventually enter.

I was stunned, and I felt robbed. That was it? She had made this dramatic production and honestly scared the wits out of me to tell me I needed to keep my faith? If anything, this was working me the other way. At that moment at the tender age of five, I realized what a sham adults had made of the church and organized religion. I also realized that only true faith comes from within. I lay awake many nights that summer trying to reconcile the fact that there were several religions with millions of followers in the world, and what if none of them were right? That meant vast amounts of people were devoting their entire lives to a lifetime of wrong-mindedness. How could that be? How could god let that happen?

It wasn't until years later that I realized that the basic tenets of all of the religions are close to being identical and that Islam, Christianity and Judaism actually share many of the same religious accounts and precepts. And as comedian Jon Stewart once said, "They all started within the same three-block radius of each other!" Of course there are similarities, yet it is the fundamentalists and fanatics who make a big deal out of the differences and incite people to kill and die for them. I always felt that many organized religions have actually thwarted the original and pure message brought forth by true prophets like Mohammed, Buddha, Jesus and Abraham. Once a religion is founded and large amounts of people get involved, agendas soon follow, and power becomes the motivating factor — not the true message of peace, tolerance, and love that is the pervasive theme in all the major religions today.

It's because of this that I always believed that true spirituality is a personal relationship between you and god, not between you and some unneeded middleman who asks you for money to continue his services to tell you how to worship and what to think.

CHAPTER 2:
THE SHAPE OF THINGS TO COME

When I was in my late twenties in the early 1990s, I quit my job as a weekly newspaper editor near the Delaware beaches and moved closer to Philadelphia to launch an entertainment magazine with a good friend and my girlfriend at the time. We started modestly by running the entire production out of the basement of a house we rented, but within two years we had established an office in Wilmington, Delaware (about half an hour south of Philly) with a staff of about a dozen.

I was also trying to pursue a career in music by heading an alternative rock band that played up and down the East Coast from New York to the Baltimore area. This combination of things put me in contact with a large amount of interesting people in the early 1990s.

Eventually, the advice my friends had given me bore itself out — *never ask a friend to be your roommate and never start a business with someone you're romantically involved with.* I ignored both rules and both relationships disintegrated after the first few years of the magazine getting started. My girlfriend and I parted ways with my friend, and then she and I split up. What made matters worse was that she and I had to continue working together for a few more years afterward. It was a painful combination of us still trying to pull together for financial reasons while also attempting to undermine each other on a personal level. Unprofessional shouting matches in front of the staff and personal taunts during deadlines were a regular occurrence.

I used to tell people it was worse than any divorce I could imagine because in most divorces, you're not financially obligated to be in the proximity of the other person on a daily basis. When we started dating other people, that brought things to a critical head, but eventually the tension wore off. She moved to the West Coast and I managed to find a buyer for the magazine a few years later.

In the months prior to me finding the interested buyer, things began to go dramatically wrong for me personally. It began as a string of things I would normally shrug off, but then it got so ridiculous it felt like outside forces were at play. I had several high-profile job offers ripped out from under me at the last minute under bizarre circumstances. On a daily basis, almost everything I did went awry to the point that I couldn't even throw something in the garbage without me missing the bucket several times and getting fully aggravated. It felt like someone or something was thwarting my every move.

It came to a head one night as I drove home late from work. I was half a mile from my house when I got pulled over by the police. I wasn't speeding, and the officer said he was making a "routine check." I waited for him to run a scan on my license and when he returned he asked me if I knew that it had been suspended. I was so used to bad luck at this point I almost wasn't surprised. A speeding ticket I had gotten in Nebraska years before during a cross-country trip had come back to haunt me. I eventually got my license reinstated by paying the fine, but I was now feeling snake bitten. What exactly was going on? Things weren't just going wrong. Everything was going wrong at every point of the day. And it felt like there was some intelligence behind it.

The next day, I was at the printer watching the latest issue of my magazine tumble off the press and making sure there were no glaring errors. These days were excruciating because I was working on very limited sleep and had to wait for four hours for the full press run to cycle through. I staggered home in the late afternoon and dropped on the bed to grab a power nap.

I lay there for a moment face down, fully clothed and just ready to drop off to sleep when I felt a presence behind me. It felt menacing and very tangible, and it loomed over me and drew closer. Then I felt something solid press up against the seat of my pants. I wasn't afraid because I was still half asleep, but I instinctively rolled over and clumsily took a swing at whatever was apparently trying to mount me. It filled me with anger and made me think there really was something lurking around that was causing all of my troubles… and it apparently wanted to molest me as well!

A few weeks later, an ex-girlfriend called me out of the blue to see how I was doing. "Not so hot," I said. "I feel like someone has put a curse on me. Everything is going wrong to the point of ridiculousness."

"I know someone who might be able to help you," she said. At this point, I was up for anything. "She does something called remote releasement and she can break curses and take negative things away."

"I'm in," I said. She gave me the number and I made the call to the woman a few hours later.

When I called I didn't know what to expect. I had never even consulted a psychic before and I was fairly skeptical about people who claimed to see spirits or know peoples' thoughts, but at this point I was so pushed to the margins that I was open to anything that might help me.

The woman was very calm and unassuming, and she explained to me that she could do all of her work remotely, hence the term "remote releasement." We didn't need to meet, she said, and that made me raise my antennae of skepticism a bit further. How credible was she? She asked me to send her a recent picture as well as one from when I was three years old, and a check for her time. It was a leap of faith, but I did it and waited for her call the next day.

She called me at the pre-arranged hour, and she wasted no time telling me that the previous night had been eventful. She also said I might feel a lack of energy or other strange symptoms over the next three days.

"So did you see anything negative around me or had someone put a curse on me?" I asked.

"You did have some negative things around you," she said. "Some of them were around you like a cage… and they were from your own thoughts and habits, so I removed those. I also scanned your astral body and found you had a build-up of some kind of greenish gunk around your testicles and that was from you having sex with women you're not in love with. I removed that, so you can have healthier sexual relationships if you choose to," she continued.

So far, I was pretty stunned.

"Did you have a grandfather die recently... like in the past few years?" she asked.

"Yes, about three years ago," I said. "Why?"

"I found a serpent coiled around your neck and the head was emerging from your mouth. When I asked who it was and why it was there, it replied, 'I'm the grandfather from the lizard side of the family. I'm here to piss the boy off.'"

A chill went up my spine because that sounded exactly like something my grandfather might say. My maternal grandfather had not liked me since birth, which my mother had revealed to me when I was an adult. There was nothing I had done to cause it; it was a disliking from the moment I was born, she said. He had obviously favored my other brothers and unfortunately, I was unaware of it until I was in my late twenties. At that time, I called my grandfather to ask for a loan to start my magazine business and he had rudely declined and then hung up on me. When I called back to find out what was going on, he started talking about my younger brothers and how they were probably going to turn out better than me. It left me feeling pretty bitter toward him, so I didn't ever really talk to him after that.

Then he died a few years later. I had no idea he had been harboring this kind of vindictiveness towards me.

The psychic said my grandfather had been the cause of most of my problems and that a curse had not been put on me. She had also removed an ancient entity that had been attracted to me when I was in the mountains on a ski trip I had taken a few years earlier. This non-human spirit had attached to me and was picking up the energy I was generating when I was partying and chasing women at the time. The combination had been draining every bit of positive energy and good luck I had.

The psychic then said that once she removed all of these things, light shot from my higher self into all directions across all space and time. She said it was like nothing she had ever seen and was so beautiful she wished she could have painted it or captured it in a photograph.

"Do you do anything creative?" she asked.

"Yes, pretty much that's how I make a living — through writing, graphic design and creating music."

"Well, that's good," she said. "That energy was a part of what creativity you'll have from now on."

It took a while for me to process all of this. I couldn't believe my grandfather had been causing my bad luck and I was so pissed off I jokingly vowed to myself that I would kick his ass whenever I died and found him on "the other side." I told a few people close to me, half expecting them to think I was losing my mind, but surprisingly everyone was extremely interested and accepting. My parents made me promise not to tell my grandmother because it would be too much for her to take.

Then, two nights later I had a physical manifestation. I awoke one morning to find myself completely soaked in fluid from head to toe. I'm guessing it was sweat because my skin felt extremely soft, like it does after you've gone for a long run or exercised very hard. But the amount released was astounding. It was as if I had wet the bed from head to toe and about a gallon of fluid had come out of every pore of my body. The bed sheets were soaked, and the wet spot radiated around my entire body and about six inches outward. I called up the psychic to tell her what had happened, and she wasn't very surprised.

"It's not unusual to have physical things happen after a remote releasement," she said. "This one was a little more dramatic than most."

Within a week of my remote releasement my luck completely changed. I had been doggedly trying to find another job and was getting shot down on every level. Suddenly, I got a call back from a local web design firm and I took the job. Six months later, I was recruited by the local daily newspaper and I ended up taking a job as the webmaster of their website. All of this enabled me to move in with my girlfriend Tracey who agreed to move out of her mother's place in central New Jersey. It took some coaxing, but we moved into a condo in Delaware together about six months from the time I had the remote releasement.

CHAPTER 3:
HEALING TOUCH

Several months after Tracey and I settled into our new place, my brother and his wife gave me a Christmas gift that had a profound effect on me: They paid for a weekend-long Reiki class. For the uninitiated, Reiki is a healing modality where the practitioner uses his/her hands to channel and move energy to places on a person's body for healing.

A few years before, when I was still working at the magazine, I had broken my ankle. Coincidently, we were doing an entire series on alternative medicine for a special issue, and I interviewed a Reiki practitioner. During the interview, the guy offered to do a free session on me and asked me if I had any ailments he could work on in particular.

"Absolutely," I said. "I've got a broken ankle."

He was up for the challenge, so one afternoon I went to the wellness center and he laid hands on me. I didn't know much about Reiki at the time other than I knew it had to do with healing touch. My preconception was that a practitioner laid hands on the afflicted area and concentrated on it, so I was a little surprised when the practitioner I was interviewing almost entirely avoided my ankle. Instead, he concentrated on my chakras and meridians (energy points and intersections on my body) and worked on getting them in balance so my body could heal itself. He did pay a few minute's worth of time on my ankle, but that was it.

The end result was I never did wear a cast, and it took about a month before I could walk normally on it again. This was a lot better than languishing in a cast for six weeks and then dealing with physical therapy for another few weeks.

After this experience, I was intrigued with the practice. It seemed a little bit like magic, but the mechanics made sense to me. There is energy flowing everywhere, including in every cell of our bodies. If someone can direct positive energy through their hands, why wouldn't it have a positive effect if applied to someone's body?

So I was curious about taking the class and wondered in the back of my mind how I could learn how to do the magic. How could someone teach you how to suddenly heal with your hands? It seemed a little bit like Star Wars where Luke learns how to use the Force.

When I arrived at the wellness center to take the class, I was surprised to see I was the only male there out of 15 people. The instructor was a little surprised, too.

"For some reason, Reiki is mainly practiced by females," she said. "So what made you come here today?"

"I've always been a manual person," I said. "I use my hands a lot. I play guitar, and I like to touch people and give massages. I also think I'm a healer."

She smiled and seemed pleased with my answer and then everyone else in the room explained their story.

The session started off a little dull. There was a lot of praying, meditating and summoning of angels. At the time I was still not open to hearing this kind of thing, so I sort of tuned it out. However, as I had my eyes closed during meditations and attunements, I kept seeing a distinct purple shape swirling in my mind's eye.

Later that day, the instructor showed us a traditional symbol that represented Reiki, and it was the exact shape I had been seeing. She also said that purple is the color of healing, so as you do Reiki with your eyes closed, it's good to see that color in your vision.

So far, I was a little intrigued but not exactly blown away. The last thing we did that day was attempt to generate some Reiki energy with our hands. This was the part of the program that seemed like teaching a Jedi how to use the Force. How could someone be taught how to do something magical?

We were all asked to stand up, bend at the knees and hold our hands out at arm's length. We were then asked to turn our palms facing each other inwardly, clench the Kegel muscles between our legs, press our tongues to the roofs of our mouths and then take a deep breath. The next thing we were supposed to feel was solid energy in between our two hands. I wasn't expecting to feel anything and the first time I tried it, nothing much happened.

But when I drew my second breath, I could feel tangible energy there. It was as if I had a roll of paper towels pressed between my hands. It was amazing. I moved my hands slightly from side to side and felt the energy move with it. I had somehow been taught the magic and I was becoming a believer.

The next day we broke into pairs and did sessions on each other, and anyone who paired with me remarked at how hot my hands were and that my touch felt electric.

In the last half of the day, we did group sessions where several people applied Reiki on a single subject. The instructor and her assistant asked if there was anyone there with a health ailment, and one woman revealed that she had fluid around her heart and was scheduled for an operation to relieve it.

The instructor's assistant and six of us worked on this woman for about half an hour. She started out lying on her stomach and after about 10 minutes the temperature of the room began to rise. As I ran my hand over the woman's heart area, it felt like my hand had fallen asleep. Uncomfortable tingling sensations erupted each time I moved over the area. The instructor told me later that this was the negative energy being drawn from the woman's affliction.

Suddenly the woman said, "I feel breath on my face," which was weird because no one was near her head.

"Those are angels," the instructor said. "It's OK."

As I looked up at the instructor, I saw a distinctly-drawn "X" on her throat. I assumed this was some arcane ritual and that she had gouged it with her own fingernail before starting the session.

The instructor moved to the woman's heart and told the woman to release the fluid. At that moment, the woman began crying uncontrollably.

"I'm releasing it through my eyes," she sobbed when she could catch her breath.

All of this was astounding to us. The air was thick with energy and there we were… a bunch of people right off the street who were engaged in some seriously intense magic. It was all very real, yet supernatural.

When the session ended, everyone's face was flushed, and we opened the doors and windows to let the air out of the room. I met the instructor in the hallway as we both got a drink of water, and I asked her about the "X" on her neck.

"What do you mean?" she asked.

"You had an "X" drawn on your neck. It's sort of fading now, but I thought you drew it." I said.

Another student came over and said she'd noticed the same thing. The instructor was a bit dumbfounded because she had been completely unaware of it. Goosebumps went up on my arms.

Then another student told us that "X" is an ancient rune symbolizing healing. No one said anything other than "wow" for about five minutes.

At the end of the day, the instructor asked me if I'd like to be a subject and I agreed. I laid on my back and six women laid their hands on me, and I felt like I was getting my batteries recharged. When the session ended, the instructor asked if anyone had had any remarkable things happen and almost every woman there said they had felt electrical jolts from my body, and one girl said she'd actually felt an arc manifest on her tongue.

The instructor looked at me and said, "You're going to be a Reiki master someday."

I took this as a compliment but didn't exactly take her remarks seriously. I had no intention of pursuing Reiki as any kind of profession, and the whole reason I had taken the session was out of simple curiosity. But the things that had transpired during the class had had their impact on me. How couldn't they? It felt like we had been bending reality.

As I got ready to leave, the Reiki Master's assistant came up to me and said, "I don't know how to tell you this, but I feel compelled to get to know you better and that I need to introduce you to a friend of mine who's clairvoyant and who does tarot readings. Are you open to meeting him?"

Whenever I'm presented with unusual requests like this, I never say no. I gave the woman my number and told her to call me whenever she wanted to introduce me to her friend.

I told Tracey about the weekend and the fact that a stranger wanted to read my tarot cards. She was up for the weirdness as well, so we all met at our condo one weekend afternoon.

The psychic was not what I would have expected a clairvoyant to look like. He was a slight man with a '70s mustache and was a heavy smoker. He looked a little down and out, but he and the Reiki Master's assistant were both extremely friendly and upbeat when they greeted us.

We all sat down at our coffee table and the psychic did his thing. He read Tracey's cards first and the first thing he said was, "You could do what I'm doing now. You have the gift. You just don't know it."

Tracey's response made everyone laugh. "But what would I do with it?" she asked with open innocence.

He told her that we would eventually be moving to a state that started with the letter "C" and that money would always be around us.

Then he did my cards. "Again," he said. "You could be doing readings as well. In fact, I feel like you'll be well known in this lifetime."

"You've had many past lives, and in one of them you were an Essene. Do you know who they were?"

I told him that I didn't.

"They were the holy men who taught Jesus when he was young, and they wrote some of the Dead Sea Scrolls," he said. "You were also a well-known holy man in a later life. I see you as an archbishop… possibly the Archbishop of Canterbury."

Then he sat silent for a while as if he were viewing some kind of scene from a movie that only he could see.

"Wow," he finally said, and he stuck out his hand to shake mine. "I'm honored to know you."

This wasn't at all how I thought the session would go. Tracey and I had expected to focus on how we would be doing at our jobs and whether we would be making more money, not that we were potentially clairvoyant or future tarot card readers.

They both left, and Tracey and I talked about the session for weeks but more out of curiosity than anything serious. Don't misunderstand, we thought it was all very cool, but we were so wrapped up in our daily comings and goings that we weren't thinking much beyond that. I eventually lost touch with my Reiki contacts as well as the psychic over the course of the next few months.

Less than a year later, I got a job offer near White Plains, NY to work for a start-up web development company. I took the position, and Tracey and I found a place to live in Connecticut… a state that starts with a "C.".

CHAPTER 4:
A STATE THAT STARTS WITH A "C"

In 1998, I was working as a webmaster for a prominent daily newspaper in Delaware during the beginning of the "Internet Gold Rush" of the late 1990s. New web companies were sprouting up every day, and investor money was being thrown at these companies without so much as a business plan or a strong idea behind them. The prevailing thought at the time was that if you dropped a lot of money on a web idea, millions of dollars would come back in return. It was almost like throwing money at the wind in the hopes that more would blow back.

Because I had a web job, I was being recruited by job headhunters on a monthly basis, so I actually had my pick of jobs that were coming my way. It was the polar opposite of my employment situation just a few years before.

I was really enjoying my webmaster job, so I was turning down most of the offers. Only a serious increase in pay would turn my head because for the first time since I sold the magazine, I was working in a position that was actually fulfilling and rewarding to me.

But after about a year and a half, I received a job offer from a start-up web development company in White Plains, NY that gave me the possibility of a 50% increase in pay. This turned my head. The big catch would be that we'd have to move out of the area.

Tracey wasn't too psyched about it when I first presented the idea to her, but she eventually warmed up to it when I told her about the pay. She had grown up in New Jersey almost her entire life, and it had been a huge leap of faith for her to move to Delaware with me. She wasn't exactly loving it in Delaware, so she felt a combination of apprehension of trying another move mixed with the desire to get the hell out of Delaware.

We took a week off and stayed at a friend's house in Connecticut to look for places to stay in the White Plains area. We were getting so discouraged looking for places to rent in the New York area that Tracey began crying one afternoon after we had taken a look at a damp apartment that was actually in someone's basement. The monthly rent was close to twice what we were paying in Delaware for our three-bedroom townhouse that had a front and backyard, and it seemed like every place we looked was worse than the last.

Then we began looking for places in Connecticut, and as we drove over the state line on the Merritt Parkway, it seemed like the clouds parted. We literally drove from the New York border that was under construction, treeless and barren, into the Connecticut border that was peppered with trees, deer, and beautiful scenery. The second we crossed the line, I thought of the psychic's prediction that we would move to a state that started with the letter "C" and I got a ripple of goosebumps.

We found a great three-bedroom house and put a deposit down on it that day. Before the realtor even showed up, Tracey and I peeked in the windows and then began high-fiving and hugging each other in the driveway. The place was exactly what we were looking for.

I gave my notice in Delaware, attended a few going-away parties, and then Tracey and I made the move. We moved into our place in November and in January I surprised Tracey by asking her to marry me in front of the clock tower in Markt Square in Brugge, Belgium at the stroke of midnight on New Year's Eve 2000. I took her there for a vacation and she had absolutely no idea what my intentions were beforehand. In fact, when I actually got down on my knee and presented the ring to her the sight was so bewildering she thought I was joking. But when she saw I was serious she burst into tears, ran to the first woman she saw in the crowded square, and showed the ring and began telling what happened. Unfortunately, this woman didn't speak English and she was terrified by Tracey's hysterics. Within a few minutes, however, the woman's daughter (who spoke English) came to the rescue and explained the situation and everyone began hugging each other. Not long after, a young British girl came up to Tracey and asked, "Excuse me, are you the girl who just got engaged?" When Tracey said that she was, the girl said, "I just got engaged right over there," and she pointed to a place about 10 yards from where I had knelt down. We ended up befriending the couple, celebrating the night with them and hanging out with them for the rest of the vacation.

Things were going well for a while. I was working out at the gym on a regular basis and taking an assortment of bodybuilding supplements like creatine and arginine to maintain my strength and physique. I got to the point where

I was bench pressing well over 300 lbs., and I could run 2 miles while only breathing through my nose. I was probably in the best shape of my life and I was in my mid 30s.

In September of 2001, Tracey and I got married on the beach in Seabright, NJ. Because it was less than three weeks after the September 11 attacks, several relatives and friends from across the country were reluctant to fly out, but even still, we had over 100 people in attendance. Tracey and I vowed not to have a traditional ceremony and reception, so we got married in the sand, and we basically had an open-mic type of music reception. I hired a friend's group to be the house band and because several of our friends are musicians, we were treated to performances all afternoon. The last band to perform was my own, and we regrouped to play two songs.

Two days later, Tracey and I flew to Bora Bora and honeymooned in an overwater bungalow that had a glass bottom so that we could see the fish below us. Even though it rained almost every day we were there, I still think it's the most beautiful place I've ever visited.

When we returned, I continued writing music, and I built a makeshift recording studio in our basement. I brewed my own beer and adopted a penchant for the semi-illegal liquor absinthe. Life was good.

But something was missing. In 2002 I felt I was at a crossroads. After making the move to New England, getting married and eventually buying a house, all the momentum had subsided. There seemed to be no forward movement anymore. It bothered me so much that I looked up the woman who had done my remote releasement years before. I told her my story and said that I felt "stuck" and asked her if she could see if there was anything holding me back on an energetic or spiritual level.

She did a reading on me and didn't see anything major. She did say that from an energetic standpoint, I was a walking paradox: I craved unbridled freedom and stability at the same time. She recommended I carry some crystals in my pocket to counter act the energetic conflict.

At this time, I began reading books like "Many Lives, Many Masters" by Dr. Brian Weiss and "Journeys Out of the Body" by Robert Monroe. The latter had the biggest impact on me. In fact, it really changed my perspective on the afterlife, the idea of god, etc. I realized that we never die and that we have a material body (the shell we walk around in on a daily basis while "alive") and we have a Higher Self. These two bodies aren't always in tune or don't always directly communicate, but it can explain where intuitive thoughts and messages come from. I also found Monroe's descriptions of traveling to Locale 2 (heaven/hell/afterlife) absolutely fascinating.

The book also reaffirmed what I had always thought… that god was more an intelligent energetic force than a robed old figure with white hair. God is the center of all energy and we each are connected to this source and have an element of godliness or godlike energetic potential in all of us.

While I was reading the book, I noticed a peculiar thing was happening to me when I slept. If I fell asleep on my back, about 15 minutes into deep sleep, my body would begin vibrating and I felt like a current of electricity was running through me. I ignored it until I read Monroe's chapter on how to have a controlled out of body experience, and then whenever I felt this happen I would try to pull myself out of my material body. It never worked until one night it happened by accident.

I was asleep on my stomach when suddenly I felt that I had detached from my body and I woke up but was still in a trance-like state. I instinctively knew once I had detached that I needed to think of a destination, and for whatever reason I chose to visit my ex-roommate Deny, a woman I had shared an apartment with for years when I ran the magazine in Delaware. She had moved to Las Vegas with her boyfriend, and I had never been to her place in person or even seen any pictures of it. In fact, I hadn't talked to Deny in months except to invite her to our wedding.

I found myself hovering in her apartment about 6 feet in the air. I looked down and could see the detail of the fibers of her gray carpet and realized I was in the middle of her living room. The TV was on, but no one was sitting on the couch directly across from it. I hovered to her bedroom and saw her lying face down in bed, tangled in her sheets.

I sent an email to her the next day, described her apartment and asked her if it was accurate. She confirmed that it was and remarked that she habitually fell asleep before her boyfriend and that he often stayed up watching TV. He must've been in the bathroom when I arrived, which would explain him not being on the couch the few minutes I was there.

I was encouraged by this experience but didn't know what to do with it. I also couldn't repeat it no matter how hard I tried. With other major distractions going on in my life, I soon forgot about trying it again.

CHAPTER 5:
UNDER PRESSURE

Around this time, pressure and stress began to mount in my life. Things were not going well at work. After working for only six months at the company that moved me to New England, I got an offer to work at a larger Fortune 500 company that seemed a lot more stable. Unfortunately, the company didn't really know what to do with a "web guy," and I sat around for months before I proposed several ideas to them and eventually transitioned into a more solid role. After two years, however, I had not gotten a promotion or anything other than a cost of living pay increase. It was the first time in my life where I felt I wasn't excelling at my job. I was a fish out of water, after all… a long-haired artist/musician in a stifling corporate environment.

To make things worse, I got passed over for a promotion when my boss took a position elsewhere in the company and though I was the heir apparent, someone else was offered the job. I didn't take this very well and there was some initial tension between us.

A few months after the dust settled, I had the uncomfortable but inevitable meeting where I asked him for a raise, pointing out that I hadn't received any kind of promotion in almost three years.

He deftly countered by telling me he didn't honestly see where I fit in his organization the next year. This rattled me pretty well. The Internet Gold Rush had gone bust, and people in the formerly-glamorous and lucrative web field were now scrambling for safety like rats on a sinking ship. Even though I hated the corporate environment, I had been wise enough to ask for a high entry salary and that was getting me through the tough times. Also, this company had been around decades before the internet and was not in any danger of folding, so I considered myself safe.

But now I had been passively-aggressively threatened by my boss and I wasn't sure if my days were numbered.

That New Year's Eve, Tracey and I spent the night partying with friends in Manhattan, and then stayed the next day to continue drinking and celebrating. The day after, I went to work but Tracey stayed home complaining of an extra bad hangover. That afternoon I got a phone call.

"Gregg, I wasn't feeling good all day, and I felt nauseous on top of it, so I decided to get a pregnancy test," Tracey said.

"What?!" I said.

"It came back positive. I think I'm pregnant."

My memory of pregnancy scares went back to the late '80s and early '90s when home pregnancy tests were about as accurate as flipping a coin. I told Tracey not to worry until she saw a doctor.

"Well, I talked to my doctor and he said the tests nowadays are almost 100% accurate. I'm not ready to be pregnant!"

"What?!" I repeated.

Tracey had gone off the pill about nine months before in hopes that one day we'd get pregnant. Her doctor predicted it might take up to two years after stopping the pill because she had been on it ever since she was a teenager. Tracey had set her expectations on a two-year timetable and wasn't ready for the responsibility yet. I was happy to hear she was pregnant but was disappointed by her reaction. I didn't know what to say to her.

Fortunately, she came around after about a week, and she more than warmed up to the idea. The pivotal point was when we got the first ultrasound picture and Tracey told me she thought she loved the little peanut already as she held and rubbed her expanding belly.

While I was extremely happy with this new development, all outside pressure began to increase. Things were uncertain at my job, and now I was expecting a child. The house we lived in would not comfortably fit a small family, so we decided to start looking for other options.

We had gotten really lucky when our landlord decided to sell us the house we were renting, and we got an amazing deal on the price. We would be able to sell it for much more and use the profit as a down payment for a larger place. But as we began looking around in Fairfield County, CT, we had to pull back our initial expectations of how much house we could afford.

After a week or two of looking at a string of dreadful houses with our realtor, I insisted we bring her back to our place. Once we walked in the door, I said to her, "See, this is what we're living in now. What we want is something better than this!"

The search lasted for several months and Tracey was extremely pregnant by the time we found an interested buyer for our place. In the meantime, we had to lower the house's price by $40,000 and we still hadn't found a house for us to move into.

One night while Tracey and I were asleep, Tracey awoke to see a very visible figure at the foot of our bed. She said it was a woman wearing a prairie skirt and bonnet, clearly from the 1800s. She was attractive, although Tracey didn't recognize her, and she was looking down most of the time, so it was hard to see her face very well. The odd thing was, she was leaning against the for-sale sign post that was in our front yard at that point in time. So, the sign post and prairie woman were all there at the foot of our bed. Tracey thought she was dreaming, rubbed her eyes and rolled over to go back to sleep, but when she looked back, everything was still there. She eventually nodded back off and that was the last she saw of the apparition. The next day, Tracey was watching a talk show where a psychic mentioned that during pregnancies, it's not uncommon for ancestors to come visit the mothers-to-be. Normally it's the recently deceased, but we were thinking this might've been a distant ancestor from the 19th century.

It was Tracey's eight month of pregnancy. The home search, work stress, and baby worries were taking their toll although I didn't know it yet. I felt as healthy as a horse and was taking vitamins and working out at least twice a week. But I began to notice a peculiar thing every time I ate a meal.

At first it started as a kind of light-headedness or fogginess about 15 minutes after I ate. I would get really spacey and feel like I had almost been drugged, and the feeling would last up to an hour. Eventually, it got worse and sometimes after eating dinner, I would collapse on the couch from headaches and fatigue.

I thought it was some sort of blood sugar issue, so I tried taking some supplements that would help me metabolize sugars better and I thought they were actually working for about a week until I slid back into the same routine of symptoms again.

It became severe enough for me to see a doctor. My general practitioner put me through a battery of tests that all came back negative. When I kept returning and complaining of the same symptoms, he asked me if I was depressed.

"Well, when I feel crappy after eating, sometimes it makes me feel bad," I admitted. "But I wouldn't say I was chronically depressed."

He didn't believe me and suggested I see a psychiatrist. I didn't take this as an insult or an assault on my sanity. I simply knew the guy was wrong.

I refused to see a shrink, however, I did go to a neurologist he recommended to almost literally get my head examined. This doctor did a sleep-deprived EEG, which is a bizarre test they do after you spend the previous day with no sleep. After you arrive, fully sleepy and worn out, they shine strobe lights at varying speeds directly in your face in an attempt to trigger a seizure. It almost worked. They also glue electrodes all over your scalp to monitor the activity, and by the time I walked out of there, I looked like an asylum escapee with my hair standing on end, and eyes at half mast. The tests came back negative.

We even did a radioactive uptake test where I had to swallow radioactive pills that tracked my thyroid's function. I asked the nurse if I would develop any super powers from it, and she laughed. The next day I was X-rayed, and she actually ran a Geiger counter over my throat to test for radiation. She also told me not to spend much time around pregnant women or small children because the radiation could be harmful.

Finally, we did a round of blood sugar tolerance tests that entailed fasting half a day and then drinking a sugar drink and then drawing blood every few hours to monitor blood sugar levels. At this point I was feeling like the tests were harsher than my symptoms and I couldn't help but think they were doing me more harm than good. They showed normal results as well.

I visited my GP after all of the tests and he had no advice for me. He said, "These tests can find the larger issues, but with your symptoms, we might have to chalk it up as 'just one of those things.'" "Besides," he added, "your symptoms aren't life-threatening, so maybe you can learn to live with them. We can do a Lyme test or an Epstein Barre test but we're operating on the fringes now."

I couldn't believe what he was telling me, and because he had been referred to me by a good friend and was actually her cousin, I decided not to let him have it verbally. So, instead I never went back again. Essentially, I fired him.

I took a break from the Western medicine approach and began to do research on the internet. I kept seeing my collection of symptoms related to candida yeast overgrowth and something called "Leaky Gut Syndrome." Apparently, so much yeast can grow in the intestinal tract that it can cause stresses and tears in the lining that ultimately leads to toxins being released into the bloodstream. Every description of it made my skin crawl. Eventually, I collected a few names of doctors who specialized in its treatment, but I shifted my concentration on finding a house to move my family.

We had zeroed in on a buyer for our current place, but there was no prospect in sight for us as far as finding a house to buy. We became emotionally attached to two places, put down offers and then were promptly outbid. Our realtor kept saying that it wasn't meant to be, but that wasn't much consolation to us at the time.

We also joked that she was going to fire us as clients. We had looked at so many houses and turned up our noses at all of them that we were surprised she was still being patient with us. Finally, it got to the point where she would call me up and tell me to drive by a place before going to the trouble of making an appointment to see the inside. She asked me to take a look at one place that was about two miles away from where we were currently living, and she didn't make much fanfare about it.

I drove by one rainy afternoon and wasn't that impressed with what I saw from my car window. I didn't even bother to get out to survey the place, but a few days later I took Tracey there and we walked around the lot. It was a bit more impressive this time in the sunshine, and we discovered that it had a decent sized backyard for a place in Fairfield County, CT. We told our realtor we were interested enough to set up an appointment, and we took a look at the place a few nights later.

As it turned out, we loved the inside and the previous owners had done wonders renovating an older home with modern upgrades. We knew we had to put down a deposit or some form of serious offer immediately. The timing couldn't have worked out better. We were scheduled to close on our current house with the new owners right around when Tracey was due to give birth, so we were able to move the date back a bit to accommodate the purchase of our new place. Arranging the details of the money exchanges, personal loans from relatives, house inspections, etc. was stressful enough and my symptoms were reaching their apex.

Plus, Tracey was ready to pop any minute. She was originally due Sept. 2, but it didn't happen for another week. On the morning in question, Tracey could tell this would be the day, so I decided to stay home from work as a precaution. She was right. At about 9:30 a.m. the first contractions started, so we went in to see the doctor a few hours later. They practically laughed at us because Tracey was nowhere near being dilated enough, but her contractions were really painful.

When we went back home, I was overcome with major fatigue. Here it was, the day my wife was about to give birth and I couldn't keep my eyes open. I actually fell asleep on one of our couches while Tracey sat in agony on the other couch, contracting as silently as she could so as not to wake me. God bless her. Finally, she couldn't take it anymore and she let out a yelp, and I jumped to my feet and drove us back to the doctor. The nurses practically laughed in our faces again when they saw we were back so soon, and then Tracey had such a powerful contraction that it made her cry right in front of them, and they totally changed their tune. They put Tracey in a wheel chair and took her to a birthing room.

Tracey's contractions were coming on strong and she was asking for an epidural when anyone resembling a nurse or a doctor entered the room. Finally, after over an hour of enduring the pain, a doctor came in to administer the anesthesia via a needle into her spine. It helped for a while, and they attached a heart monitor to her stomach to watch the baby's heart rate and another sensor on her chest to monitor hers.

I held her hand and gave her bottled water for a while, and then when the excitement died down, I pulled some cushions off of a chair and made a makeshift bed on the floor. The fatigue was hitting me again so for the next few hours I caught naps in between running for food and waiting things out.

In the middle of one of my naps, Tracey started moaning like she had at home. Either the epidural was wearing off or her contractions were so strong they were pounding through the anesthesia. I went to Tracey's side and kept my eyes on the heart monitors and made sure they were in the normal ranges where the doctor said they should be.

Within an hour, Tracey was trying to make the move to push the baby out. Each time she had a contraction and pushed, I watched the baby's heart rate drop dramatically. The doctor noticed it as well and said that the umbilical cord was probably wrapped around the baby's neck. As Tracey tried to push her further down the birth canal, the cord was wrapping tighter and strangling the baby. Each time the contractions and pushing occurred, the heart rate would drop until every medical staff in the room began to worry.

But Tracey was making progress. The baby's head finally crowned at one point, and I thought it would actually slide right out like I had seen in the training films. But, no. The doctor came in and tried applying a suction cup to the top of the baby's head, and I couldn't believe what a flimsy contraption it was. I was expecting some sort of high-end medical suction device, but this thing looked like it had been purchased at a local hardware store. After two more attempts with the suction, the doctor said this was it. Tracey HAD to get the baby out or else... or else WHAT I didn't know. The baby was too far down the birth canal for a C-section, and it was apparently stuck with its cord wrapped around its neck and couldn't survive for much longer.

They tried propping Tracey upright and when she pushed, some brown fluid came out. At first, they thought it was a bowel movement, but I could see that there were large cells floating in the secretion. This was *meconium* and I knew about this. It is the baby's first bowel movement and if the baby inhales it in the womb, it can cause brain damage.

I almost passed out at this point but not from being squeamish of the meconium. It was entirely out of stress.

The doctor began yelling at Tracey to push, and Tracey asked if it was possible for her to pass out while she was lying down. I could see all the blood rushing from her face, but when the next contractions came, she somehow managed to get the baby out. Afterwards, she said she felt like she had had some kind of help... from where she didn't know, but she distinctly felt the presence of her dead grandmother during the last push.

Prior to this day, I used to fantasize about how I would welcome my offspring into the world, and it involved me cutting the umbilical cord and holding the baby up to the heavens while still covered in birthing goo. But as soon as the baby came out, the doctors shoved me aside and cut the cord themselves. The baby's body looked green and she was making little coughing and groaning sounds in between cries.

It was a strange thing. Tracey and I knew there was something wrong with her immediately and it caused us not to bond with her out of some sort of weird animal instinct. I've talked to other people who have gone through a similar experience of not getting attached to a baby who had health problems at birth. Perhaps it's nature's way of lessening the impact if something goes wrong.

I left Tracey to get stitched up in the delivery room and went with a doctor who washed off my daughter and did some tests on her. He wanted to keep her in the natal intensive care unit for a few days. She had inhaled some meconium and had taken on some fluid in her lungs. Her oxygen level wasn't where it should be either. I was bracing myself for any effects of brain damage.

The doctors moved Tracey into a recovery room, and I met her there and spent the night. A doctor popped his head in at 3 a.m. to tell us our daughter was doing better, and Tracey riddled him with questions about brain damage and other possible ill effects of the traumatic birth. The doctor did everything short of guarantee that she would be OK, and we went back to sleep.

The next morning, we visited Carly in the NIC (Neonatal Intensive Care) unit, and we noticed that they had a rule that you couldn't mention the child's real name in the unit.

This was another way of keeping the caregivers from getting too attached to babies who might not make it. Lucky for us, Carly was doing much better and we were able to hold her. She had an IV attached to her arm and her little mouth was wide open like a baby bird looking for food.

Later that morning, I went to go get breakfast for us and when I returned, I'll never forget the scene I came upon. There was Tracey quietly breast feeding our daughter for the first time. My heart almost exploded from good emotions.

A day later we were able to take Carly home for the first time. But things didn't exactly settle down. In a month, we would be selling our house, buying a new one and moving into the new place. It was a nightmare of coordination as anyone knows who has gone through this experience, but it was tempered with the fact that we were brand new parents with a month-old baby and Tracey was feeling the first effects of postpartum depression.

My symptoms were beginning to rage at this point as well. One day when my father and I were coordinating with a contractor to get our hardwood floors refinished, we grabbed lunch at a local Mexican place. I ate a burrito, and for some reason I was overcome with so much fatigue that I had to lie down and take a nap in the back of our SUV. This was my alarm bell because this wasn't like me at all. My parents were both in denial. My dad laughed, "I feel like I need to take naps after eating, too." But this was totally different. I didn't FEEL like I needed to take a nap, I HAD to find a place to lie down or I would've collapsed.

CHAPTER 6
MYSTERY ILLNESS

I spent the next few months researching on the web about my symptoms and I kept seeing issues around yeast overgrowth and "Leaky Gut Syndrome." I managed to find a Leaky Gut specialist in Manhattan who was also a naturopath. This appealed to me because at this point I was losing my faith in traditional/Western medicine based upon past experience.

I never did see the doctor in person, which was fine by me. We conducted all appointments on the phone and his office sent me weekly testing equipment, so I could do my own urinalysis and gauge my progress. The course of treatment included all manner of strong herbal and vitamin remedies, and I stayed on the protocol for about a year. At the end of that time I barely felt any difference, and in fact, I was concerned that I might actually be feeling slightly worse. To top it off, none of the treatments, testing supplies or appointments were covered by my health insurance plan. I had literally spent thousands of dollars and ended up at square one... possibly even square minus-one.

During my last appointment with the doctor, I asked him why I was having persistent yeast issues. Certainly, there was something that was the root cause. He was convinced I had higher than average amounts of metal in my system and that this was causing the issue. He suggested I might consider having my amalgam fillings removed, and I began chelation therapy, which attempts to leech the metal toxins out of your system through pills.

I began to lose faith in this doctor as well, and Tracey was particularly skeptical of him. I was discouraged enough to go back to my GP and ask for a recommendation for a gastroenterologist. The guy he recommended turned out to be one of the worst doctors I've ever seen.

When I met with this doctor, his attitude and ego entered the room before he did. He took one look at me and said, "You don't *look* sick," and then he asked me what the problem was. I told him about the symptoms I had every time I ate and that I had been seeing a naturopath to treat Leaky Gut Syndrome.

"What the hell *is* Leaky Gut Syndrome?" he asked me skeptically. I couldn't believe he was a gastroenterologist and was unfamiliar with it, and I had never had a doctor question whether or not I was sick based upon my outward appearance.

When I started to explain the details, he looked at me and said, "So, did you learn all of this off the internet?"

Then, things started to get contentious. We argued about yeast overgrowth and he insisted he do an endoscopic exam which would entail putting me under general anesthesia, shoving a tube down my throat and cutting a piece of my intestines for a biopsy. This sounded like the most invasive test yet, and there was no way I was going to do it. So, instead, he gave me a rectal exam for no apparent reason.

I walked out of there dazed and pissed off. Weeks later, a friend at work highly recommended a gastroenterologist in Manhattan and I had a similar experience. The difference was this doctor was a very nice guy, but he also "didn't believe" in Leaky Gut Syndrome. His only way of testing was through endoscopy, and he made a very telling and all-to-familiar comment. "So, your symptoms aren't life threatening. Maybe you try to live with them…"

That was all I had to hear, and I never returned to either doctor.

I was running out of ideas. I did a wide search on the internet for thyroid doctors, holistic doctors, and naturopaths in my general area, and I had weeded it down to two.

The first was a holistic naturopath who I thought was going to save the day. When I called to make an appointment, his receptionist did a fantastic job convincing me that the symptoms I was describing were very treatable and that the doctor was practically a miracle worker. But there were a few catches. The first appointment was basically an all-day interview and testing session that would cost about $1,000 and wasn't fully covered by my insurance plan. Naturopaths were considered "out of network" and my insurance would only pay for about 40% of the charges.

I felt like I had no choice, so I kept the appointment. On the day in question, I sat in his office waiting for him to enter, and my eye wandered to the framed diploma on his wall. I was a bit unnerved to see that he had gotten his medical credentials in a third world country. I tried to put this out of my mind and was pinning my hopes on the fact that his combination of holistic medicine matched with naturopathy would get to the root of what was ailing me.

The appointment was grueling, and more than 10 vials of blood had to be drawn from me. In the middle of the blood letting I suddenly began feeling faint and thirsty at the same time. "I feel like I'm gonna pass out," I told the male nurse. At first, he thought I was joking and said, "C'mon, you're a big guy. You can take it." But then he took a look at my face, and he got me a glass of water and helped me get horizontal on the examining table. It was weird and made me think there was more wrong with me than I knew.

Then I was subjected to an allergy test that involved injecting me with small levels of toxins and allergens to see my reaction. When it was over, I had about 20 needle pricks in my triceps, some of which stained my skin for months.

After all these tests, I scheduled a meeting with the doctor to go over the results. My thyroid was fine, he said. I had no blood sugar issues, I wasn't allergic to anything major (other than dust mites and yeast), and I showed slightly higher-than-average levels of mercury and arsenic in my system. He recommended doing IV chelation therapy to get rid of the metals.

So, once a week, I went to his office, got hooked up to an IV and sat for about an hour while chelation chemicals and vitamins coursed through my veins. I got a mild case of phlebitis during one visit and on another occasion, I had a vasovagal reaction where I felt like I was going to pass out during the therapy.

I gave this a whirl for about three months and noticed that I wasn't feeling any better. I looked through my list of doctors and remembered that I had one left from my original online search, so I made an appointment with a thyroid doctor who had a naturopath on staff.

It was May 2005 and I had gone for two years without being able to find out what was going on with me. Any diagnosis outside of cancer or AIDS would be welcome. I met with the naturopath first, but beforehand she asked me to keep a daily journal of my symptoms. On the day we met, I handed her a week's worth of entries. I also described some other ongoing issues, and she looked at my blood work and urinalysis from the other doctors.

"It looks like you have Lyme disease," she said confidently. "Your cholesterol is high, and you eat right and work out, so that shouldn't be. Coupled with all of these non-specific symptoms, that's a clue." I felt a wave of initial relief. She was so sure of her diagnosis that she was prepared to prescribe antibiotics on the spot. The MD walked in and concurred. They both also recommended a Lyme test through a specific lab.

"Have you ever had a Lyme test before?" they asked. I told them I had had one two years before and that it had come back negative from a particular lab. They confirmed that the lab in question was notorious for false negative results.

They were prepared to give me doxycycline, but because I was leaving on vacation to Cabo San Lucas the next day and that doxycycline intensifies the sun's rays and can cause severe sunburns, I decided to start upon my return. I felt liberated with the knowledge that I could begin treating and attacking a tangible disease. Little did I know what kind of battle I was about to engage.

CHAPTER 7:
THE BATTLE BEGINS

Tracey and I got on a plane with our friends and flew to Cabo to spend a week at their time share on the beach. I was relieved and was actually looking forward to getting on medication, but I figured this was the last blast of partying I would have for a while. I had heard treatment of Lyme could last for a long time and I wasn't sure when I'd be able to drink alcohol again.

Not that I was able to drink much of it anyway. One of my major symptoms was the fact that I had become very sensitive to any kind of alcoholic beverages. The New Year's Eve before, I had drunk two glasses of champagne and a small glass of absinthe and I practically passed out before midnight. On another occasion, I drank three beers at dinner one night and I woke up at 4 a.m. throwing up. This wasn't like me at all. I had been known to knock back at least 10 beers without feeling any ill effects, and I had polished off 5-6 glasses of absinthe in a sitting before feeling the need to find a place to get a grip on the floor.

I paced myself by drinking a Mexican beer here and there and drank a mojito one night. We spent a lot of time in the sun during the day and the time share had a great pool. One day before dinner, I laid down for a short nap after taking a shower and I felt someone shake my legs to wake me up. When I raised my head, I didn't see anyone there. This reminded me of the experience I had in Delaware years before, but this time the nudge felt benevolent. I got the impression that someone didn't want me to be late for dinner.

Later that night, we all went out to a local restaurant and we asked a waitress to take a picture of the four of us. When we got home and developed the pictures, I noticed a distinct "orb" around my head. We have a number of pictures like these that we've collected throughout the years. With the advent of digital photography, these orbs are showing up more and more in photos. They look similar to lens flares, the circular blurs you see when too much light refracts on your camera lens, but they are different in shape and often show up in dark areas where there is no reflection happening. By all accounts, these orbs are a reflection of spiritual energy that is present.

Apparently, on this night, some sort of spirit was following me around.

As soon as we returned, I made a second appointment with the doctor and soon began taking doxycycline. Within days my symptoms intensified. I had major episodes of headaches, mental fogginess and fatigue. After a few weeks, I went back to see the doctor and he asked how I was feeling.

"Like shit!" I said.

"Good," she laughed. "It means the antibiotics are working. As they destroy the cell walls of the bacteria, the toxins from the bacteria are released into your bloodstream. Once you stop feeling bad, we can take you off the meds."

I toughed it out for almost two months and visited the doctor for a blood test to monitor my progress. On around the sixth week, I noticed some slight pain in my lower right back area where my kidneys are, and I had some sort of mild skin eruptions on top of my shoulders. I felt like I was making a breakthrough at this point, but when I got my blood test results back, the naturopath entered the room with a long face.

"You've got abnormally high creatinine levels in your bloodstream," she said. This means something could be wrong with your kidneys."

I had been taking *creatine*, which is a different compound used for body building and I asked her if that could have affected things. The thing is I stopped taking it before going on the meds, so I had not been on it for more than six weeks. She said she wasn't sure, but her theory was that my kidneys were simply being overworked by the amount of toxins they were processing and there wasn't any need for alarm. The MD, on the other hand thought that my body might be reacting to the antibiotics in an adverse way and that my kidneys could be shutting down, which was very serious obviously. I had an intuitive feeling that he was wrong, and I wanted to stay on the meds. In fact, I had been hearing about PICC lines (peripherally inserted central catheter) and I asked him about going on one. He said they were drastic and that we should try to fight the disease through oral meds, but for now I should go off of them to see if my kidneys could bounce back.

I was frustrated. I really felt like I had been making some progress, but now my MD was wimping out. He told me he would not put me back on the meds unless I consulted a kidney specialist at Yale Hospital. This set me back even more. By the time I made the appointment and visited the doctor, three weeks had passed.

The specialist took one look at me and said, "No wonder your creatinine levels are high. You're in good physical shape. You've got a higher than average amount of muscle mass for your age, and that accounts for the high levels of creatinine in your blood. Your antibiotics could've caused this to increase, but that's normal. You're safe to go back on the doxycycline."

But when I called the MD back, he was still reluctant. "I really like you and I appreciate the fact that you finally found out what was wrong with me, but I'm afraid I'm going to have to look for another doctor," I told him. He understood.

So, Tracey found a doctor in Stratford, CT who would install a PICC line for me. I felt very confident about all of this. A giant blast of intravenous meds would certainly get to the root of the problem.

This new doctor was very cautious as well and he told me he would not keep the line in for more than four weeks. I had read of people keeping lines in for more than a year and I asked him about that.

"There are two schools of thought for Lyme treatment," he said. "The conservative and the progressive. The conservatives believe you shouldn't be on antibiotics of any kind for more than a month and that's enough time to kill all the Lyme bacteria. The progressives believe that you stay on the meds until you feel better. The problem with that is some people never feel better and they end up compromising their immunes systems or damaging their organs."

I was hoping that I would feel better in the four-week span and that it wouldn't be an issue. Neither he nor any one in his office went into detail about how the line would be installed, but he told me that I would need to come back to his office once per week to get the dressing cleaned and to get my IV bags and supplies.

I thought the line would be installed in his office and was surprised when he made an appointment for me at a local hospital. I checked in and got my hospital bracelet, which felt weird. I wasn't going in for any major surgery, right?

It was August 31, 2005, and I sat for hours in the waiting room and was actually anxious to get this going. Finally, after about two hours a young doctor entered and told me he was required to explain the procedure to me. He talked of a line that would go into my arm and he was making motions toward the heart area but never actually said anything about the line going up that far. He asked me which arm I would like it in and because I'm right handed, I told him I'd like it in my left arm. He said that because the way the veins are configured over the heart that that would actually be a bit more difficult, but they would do it.

He left, and I sat there for almost another hour. What the hell had he been talking about with the veins over the heart? Wasn't this simply a shunt that would stick right out of my arm and only go in a few inches?

The doctor returned and directed me toward an operating room. I laid down on the table and noticed that there were five people in the room. Why were there so many doctors there for such a simple procedure? A nurse positioned some X-ray monitors right above my head, and a young Asian doctor entered and introduced himself. He looked at me and said that he'd be going with the biggest size of line they had. They strapped my left arm to an extension of the table and draped it with surgical cloths. Then they injected my left bicep with lidocaine. The main doctor was complaining that my arm muscles were causing trouble with the line installation, and I joked, "What's the matter, are my arms too massive for you?" This immediately brought back a memory of me watching Steve Prefontaine race Lasse Veran in the Olympics on TV when I was a kid. While they were running, the announcer described a stomach operation Veran had had and the doctors experienced difficulty in cutting through Veran's dense muscles during the procedure. At the time, that captured my imagination that Veran was that strong and tough. I laughed inwardly to myself and made the mental connection. Then I felt blood running down the part of my arm that hadn't been numbed by the injection.

And suddenly, I started feeling weird. Even though I was lying down, I felt like I might pass out and I began feeling really bad in general. I told the nurse, who was standing to my right, and the doctor performing the operation started to laugh. "C'mon, you're not going to pass out on me, are you?" But the nurse said something that changed everyone's mood instantly. Apparently, my blood pressure was dropping dramatically. Little did I know but the line was invading my heart and the doctor had actually put it in too far.

The nurse tried to take my mind off of the issue by telling me to focus on the monitor. I really hadn't been paying attention before, but there was my chest cavity in full view with a tiny wire snaking through the veins around my heart. That alone made me want to pass out, so I turned my head and tried to keep it together.

The doctor said that it was common for guys who worked out and were bigger to have vasovagal reactions, but I wasn't sure that's what was happening.

They finished up and decided to keep me an extra hour for observation. They even ordered me lunch which I ate in the hallway while semi reclining on my gurney. I felt like I was on display as the various hospital staff walked by me and stared.

I looked down at my arm and the results of the operation and couldn't believe that they had actually stitched the plastic base to the line directly to my skin so that it wouldn't move. "How fucking barbaric," I thought. It was caked with dried blood and looked terrible.

I drove to the doctor's office to get my first dose of meds and was introduced to a nurse whom I would be seeing every week. I told her about the drama around my procedure and she was surprised to hear it. "We've never had a problem like that before," she said.

She then showed me how to administer the IV antibiotics and warned me that I might have a reaction as the antibiotics began to take effect. She was right, and I began feeling headachy and fatigued. I drove home feeling fine, but when I returned I retreated to the couch and slept.

Later that night as I was sleeping in my bed, I rolled over on my left side and something terrible happened. By rolling over, I had shifted where the line was and apparently it jabbed into my heart. My heart began palpitating like crazy and this commotion woke me up. I felt like I was having some kind of heart failure. I didn't even wake Tracey up, but I went downstairs and laid on my back on the couch to see if I would die. I had a bizarre claustrophobic-type feeling and I wanted to rip this invasive piece of apparatus right out of me. It felt alien and unhealthy for me, and I lay awake the rest of the night completely frustrated and wondering if I would have another attack.

I was supposed to give an important presentation at work the next day, but I was so out of it and concerned for my life that I didn't even call in sick. Instead, I called an emergency on-call doctor to see if this experience was normal. The doctor said that it wasn't normal and that I should get the line out if it happened again, but he confided in me that it is a big deal to remove and then re-install a line. "You should tough it out if you can," the on-call doctor said.

So, I toughed it out. But the palpitations kept happening… not as bad as the original ones, but I learned not to sleep on my side anymore. My general health and mental state began to decline as well. The nurse had warned me against lifting more than 10 lbs. with my left arm when I was working out. Working out? Who could work out under these circumstances? It was all I could do to go to work during the day and then after eating dinner, I couldn't stay awake. Working out was a distant memory and I'm sure my health suffered even further as a result. I had not skipped working out with weights for more than three months since I was about 14 years old.

My mood also became darker. I was never one to feel sorry for myself, but I kept asking myself what I had done to deserve this. Plus, I would go through phases of fantasizing about shooting myself in the head to relieve the pain, pressure, and mental fog. I wasn't even suicidal. I didn't want to do it by my own hand but having my life end was sounding more and more attractive to me.

My relationship with Tracey began to suffer as well. As my moods changed, I became difficult to be around. It was hard for me to pay attention to her and very difficult to follow her stream-of-consciousness conversations. She would get mad at me for not listening or forgetting something she had said, and I would be powerless to defend myself. I simply didn't have the energy. I would also snap at her if she didn't hear something I said. It was so difficult just to get the words out that if I had to repeat it, it would infuriate me. Added to the equation was Carly. She was becoming a handful... very high maintenance and always wanting attention. It didn't take long for her to go into a crying jag if something didn't go her way.

One Christmas when Carly was just a few years old, Tracey and I began to really getting into it. On Christmas Eve, Tracey and I had a shouting match that ended with each of us yelling, "Fuck you!" to each other before going to bed. It was sad. To try to add some levity to the situation the next morning I wrote on the gift tag of one of the presents I gave her: "To: Bitch, From: Asshole." It lightened the mood somewhat, and Tracey got a good laugh out of it.

But even after Tracey snapped out of her funk, I plunged deeper into my own. I was in a tailspin that was coupled with mild depression, anti-social behavior and general feelings of hopelessness. As a defense mechanism, Tracey began to pull back from me and this caused me to resent her. At times when we weren't arguing, I'd go to her for comfort, but she'd still be licking her wounds from some past scrape we had had. It didn't leave any time for healing and reconciliation.

During this time, I also developed a dangerous CDIFF (Clostridium difficile) infection while still on the PICC line and my doctor recommended oral antibiotics to fight it. It was a lower bowel infection caused by the antibiotics from the PICC line and I was wiping out the good bacteria in my intestines without replenishing it. The treatment brought on debilitating hemorrhoids and my lowest mental state yet, and one afternoon all I could do was lie on the floor of our shower, crying in a painful fetal position.

Needless to say, I was at the end of my rope by the time my PICC line was removed after six weeks. I went to an acupuncturist hoping that I had killed all bacteria but just needed to detox. After a few weeks I stopped going because I didn't' feel any major improvements.

On a fluke, while I was at a dentist appointment that December, I was telling my dentist my tales of woe and he recommended a well-known progressive Lyme specialist right in our area. I took down the number, thanked him profusely and gave the doctor a call.

CHAPTER 8:
STAGE TWO OF THE BATTLE

The first visit with my new Lyme doctor was like going to see a therapist. In fact, I believe before he began specializing in Lyme treatment he was exclusively a neuro-psychiatrist. He had a disarming personality and looked a little bit like the actor Max Von Sydow with a gray beard. He sat me down and asked me to describe all of my symptoms and how I felt about them, and at the end of the discussion, he turned to me with a quizzical look and asked, "So what would YOU like to do?" Never in my life had a doctor asked me this question.

I told him that based upon my drastic experience with a PICC line, I would prefer not to go down that path again. He told me that based upon a set of tests he was prescribing for me that intravenous treatment might be indicated. "But we've got some alternatives," he said reassuringly.

In the meantime, he was concerned about fighting my mental fogginess, slight depression and anxicty. He prescribed a number of vitamin supplements and also put me on an oral antibiotic to begin fighting the Lyme.

A few weeks later, I went to the local hospital for a SPECT scan (Single Photon Emission Computed Tomography). A radioactive agent was injected into my arm and then I laid down while a camera rotated around my body to monitor the amount of oxygen flow that was going to my brain. The results showed that a significant part of my left frontal lobe was being affected by the disease.

When I returned to the doctor's office to discuss the results, he told me the news I was hoping not to hear. "You really should be on a PICC line," he said.

"What's the alternative?" I asked.

"We can give you weekly injections of bicillin. They are painful intramuscular injections administered with a long needle, and sometimes they are so painful we inject patients with lidocaine before the bicillin."

I laughed. Wasn't there any Lyme treatment that wasn't invasive, painful, or dangerous?

"It's either this or the PICC line," he smiled ruefully.

So, I opted for the injections. I went in every Friday afternoon for 16 weeks and had both ass cheeks shot with the painful meds by the doctor's assistant.

The injections weren't as bad as I thought they'd be during the actual injection procedure, but it was painful for me to sit down for days afterward. It was as if I was getting caned on the butt every week.

The meds also played havoc with my moods and mental clarity, which I half expected. In an effort to up the ante, the doctor put me on two more oral antibiotics at the same time. One of these, minocycline, almost caused me to go suicidal. I consulted with the doctor and his assistant separately about it and they both agreed that my negative symptoms might be signs of a Jarrish-Herxheimer reaction. Commonly called a Herxheimer reaction or "herxing," this term refers to the increased intensity of symptoms that occurs when medicine causes the destruction of bacteria and subsequent release of toxins in the bloodstream. In my case this meant headaches that made me weak and nauseous, extreme fatigue, intense mental fogginess and difficulty speaking, anti-social feelings, and depression.

The depression made all of the above symptoms much worse, and I couldn't help feeling that taking the minocycline was not only intensifying it, but possibly doing it without fighting the Lyme effectively. But there was no proof other than my intuitive feeling.

I was almost debilitated at this point. I would barely speak to Tracey in the morning, and then I would struggle through my work day. It was like spinning the Wheel of Symptoms. I never knew exactly what I'd get. Would it be paralyzing depression? Difficulty in speaking and fear of being in a room with a group of people? Fogginess that would leave me wondering where I was? Fatigue beyond belief? All of the above?

I was totally drained by the time I got home from work, and then I would routinely have a reaction to eating dinner that sapped the remainder of my energy. I would retreat to the couch and Tracey would be sullen from my lack of interaction with her. Sometimes I would even fall asleep before Carly, and she would cover me with a blanket and kiss me on the face. "Doddy sad," she said one night when she was a little more than two years old. The whole thing was sad.

I would wake up on the couch at one in the morning, sometimes from a crushing Herxheimer headache and retreat to bed with Tracey. The next morning, I would feel good for the first half hour upon rising and then the day would kick into the same old grind. It was a terrible life style and I can't believe I endured it for so long without cracking up... until I finally did.

One night in March of 2006, Tracey and I were sitting on the couch watching TV and we got into an argument. I don't remember what it was about, but it caused her to storm upstairs, and I sat there feeling defeated, lonely and unloved. I knew in my heart that Tracey loved me, but she had put up so many defense mechanisms and psychological barriers that she rarely showed me any kind of kindness or affection throughout the course of the day. The peck on the lips I got every morning was the extent of any displays of affection.

I mulled this over and decided I would go upstairs to propose an armistice. I was pissed off after our argument too, but it was unhealthy for us to go on this way. It was also unhealthy for me to be going through so much stress at work only to come home to even more of it. I figured I would appeal to Tracey's softer side and simply propose we forget about the whole thing and try to start from scratch.

I walked upstairs, and Tracey was in front of the mirror in our bathroom getting ready for bed. I stumbled on my words and managed to try to propose a truce, and she just glared at me. I said something like, "Let's just hug each other and drop all of this shit."

She leveled me with a cold look, obviously still fuming about our argument, and firmly said, "NO."

Something snapped in me like I've never felt. I plunged both hands into my hair and began pulling it and making weird groaning noises. I stumbled back and reeled around our bedroom, punching the air. I think I said something to Tracey, but I don't know what it was. At first she might've thought I was kidding, but I didn't stick around long enough to explain myself. I felt like a door had shut in my face and once again I was left to deal with my predicament alone.

I went downstairs and spent the night in our guest bedroom. As I lay on my stomach in complete depression, my heart began to palpitate wildly. For the first split second it pissed me off, but then I said out loud, "Bring it the fuck on. Take me now, God. I don't want to take my own life, but if you could take it for me, that would be good. I've done everything I can in this lifetime. I'm ready for the next…"

I fell asleep that night in the worst depression I have ever experienced. It was the utter low point in my life.

CHAPTER 9:
EVERYTHING CHANGES

The next few weeks were a blur, but I do remember catching a presentation that was being given by Dr. Wayne Dyer on a PBS TV station one day. We had the television idly on in our bedroom, when I became transfixed with what Dyer was saying. His message was that each individual's power of thought can shape that person's life. If a person concentrates on positive thinking and pursuits, then positive things and people will be attracted to that person. The reverse happens if a person is thinking negatively.

"When you change the way you look at things, the things you look at change" was his catchy quote, and these words struck such a chord in me that I bought his book "The Power of Intention." I totally absorbed its general message that thoughts are extremely powerful, and they can shape your destiny.

As a result, I began actively trying to keep my thoughts on a positive bent. This was difficult with the negative chemicals that were being generated by the minocycline, so

I asked the physician's assistant if it would be OK to discontinue. She agreed because I had been on it quite a while and I was still taking other antibiotics to fight the bacteria.

I felt like I was at a crossroads again in my life and whenever I've felt this way, I've contacted the woman who did the original remote releasement on me. I'd gotten an email from her a few weeks earlier telling me that she now did tarot readings. I made an appointment with her and we did our session over the phone.

I asked her about my health and what the future looked like, what my career path would be and how things looked for my family situation.

She said I would meet a woman who would help with my healing.

"No, maybe it's a man," she corrected herself. "Or no, a woman. Maybe it's an effeminate man… possibly even gay. Whatever the case, this person will help look after your health."

At the end of the session, she recommended I contact a woman who ran a clinic in the area that specialized in a certain type of sound therapy. In a nutshell, it is a form of treatment that relies on sound frequencies to adjust the body. The idea is that different substances have specific frequencies, and by listening to certain frequencies you can have a powerful effect on the body without depending on invasive procedures or synthetic medicines. This sounded exactly like what I needed. She gave me the number and said that this might possibly be the woman who could help with my healing, so I made an appointment.

I drove to the sound therapy center one afternoon and met with the staff. A young woman greeted me and told me she was the one who would be doing my sounds. I met with her in her office and I told her about my medical history. When I went into the story about my botched PICC installation and how the line had jabbed my heart, she gasped. I thought to myself, "She's very empathetic and is going to take good care of me."

She took a 40-second recording of my voice for analysis. I was so foggy and tired from my symptoms that when she asked me to speak uninterrupted for 40 seconds straight, I couldn't think of anything to say. "Tell me about your daughter, "she smiled. So, I did and she told me that I would need to make a follow-up appointment. The next step was for her to analyze the frequencies in my body that were out of balance in my voice and then she would test a collection of sounds on me. Based upon my reaction, she would make a final recording of sounds to give my body positive results. I made my appointment and was scheduled to come back almost two weeks later.

The next week while I was driving to the doctor's office for more bicillin injections, I had my car radio tuned to a local Manhattan rock station. The show I was listening to was a comedy talk show that I had heard several times before, but on this day the show's two co-hosts were interviewing a psychic and spiritual healer. I usually didn't pay a lot of attention to this kind of programming but something about it caught my ear. Part of it was how unusual it was for a show like this that usually featured "shock jock" programming to seriously have a guest who was promoting positive thought and spirituality. What was even more surprising was the fact that several of the more skeptical callers phoned in and began to taunt the psychic, but he pulled facts out of the air and told the hecklers extremely personal things about their lives without any prior knowledge. The incredulity on the other end of the line was so sincere, I knew the psychic was no fake. But when he began to push healing energy to these people over the phone and they exclaimed that they could feel, I was totally intrigued.

During the commercial break, they mentioned that the psychic would be in the New York metro area and would be accepting appointments. I surprised myself by writing down the number before going in for my injections. I actually called later in the day and made an appointment. I figured I had nothing to lose.

I didn't have many expectations before the call. By this time, I had had enough appointments with psychics, spiritual healers and alternative practitioners that I figured I knew what was going to happen. He'd look into my future, find any negative "attachments" and get me pointed in the right direction. Hopefully, he'd be able to shed some light on my path to healing.

I called the psychic's office on the day of the appointment and they said he was running a half an hour late. Apparently, he had all of his appointments back to back so if one ran long, it pushed all others back as well.

After an hour, his office called to tell me it would be another half an hour before he could call me. They said he was tending to a woman who was "in crisis." I didn't know exactly what that meant, but I selfishly wondered if he was going to have any energy left when he got to me.

After waiting more than an hour and a half, I finally got the call from the psychic. He apologized, and we immediately dove in. He asked me one or two questions, like why I had called and what my major issues were, but as soon as I started talking he stopped me.

"You've got A LOT of stuff going on," he said. "Wait a minute while I get rid of some of your attachments. You have a legion of negative spirits and entities attached to you."

Great, I thought. This sounded worse than simply having my grandfather attached to me.

For the next several minutes, the psychic talked to me on the phone while simultaneously removing entities. At times he would mutter something to himself or possibly to another being.

At one point I heard him say, "He's more special than you know."

"What did you say?" I asked.

"I'm getting the message that you're more special than I know. You are like one of ten people in the world," he said. "You have the ability to be doing what I'm doing."

I didn't quite know how to take these words, so I remained silent.

He then told me he had removed hundreds of entities from me and that he had destroyed some sort of ancient impediment that he had cracked away from me. Apparently, it had been placed there by some malevolent force and had remained on my spirit for thousands of years.

"I got the message that I'm the only one who could've removed it," he said. "I'm not saying that out of ego…

that's what I was told. As soon as I removed it, hundreds of angels began rejoicing. You're like family in heaven. You have some sort of connection there."

Now I really didn't know what to think because I was experiencing physical changes as well. My vision became brighter and most of my major symptoms had simply evaporated. My depression and emotional baggage of the past two years was completely lifted. I was focusing on this and not really taking in the gravity of what he was saying.

"I see you've had a past life on the planet Maldek," the psychic said. "Do you know anything about it?"

"What? No." I said.

"Look it up when you get a chance. It's a planet that used to exist next to Mars about 500,000 years ago. In fact, Mars was a water planet just like Earth and was a moon of Maldek. The larger planet was destroyed in a war, kind of like in the movie 'Star Wars,' and not only did the war decimate Maldek (which is an asteroid belt today), it destroyed most of the surface of Mars."

All of this sounded crazy to me, but I couldn't ignore the continued physical improvement I was feeling.

"It's great to know you," he continued. "You are part of the team. You need to write a book and start fighting the good fight," he laughed.

The session lasted well over an hour and he was so exact in his knowledge of me that he actually described how I looked without ever having seen me in person.

At one point while I was on the phone in my basement studio, I heard Tracey and Carly come blustering in the house. Carly was crying at the top of her lungs and Tracey was yelling at her for misbehaving. This seemed like a good time to ask about my family.

He took an astral look at Tracey and said, "Oh, she's beautiful… and she's a freak like you!" He laughed, "She's got the same abilities, and your daughter's even more powerful. She'll surpass us all someday. Of course she will; she's your daughter."

Suddenly it dawned on me. Perhaps he was the one the woman psychic had seen in her tarot reading.

I blurted out, "Can I ask you a question? Are you gay?"

He paused for a second and said, "Yes, I have had relationships with men, but I've also had relationships with women. Why?"

And I told him about the woman psychic's prediction. "She's pretty accurate," he said.

"Now you need to work on your own abilities. You need to protect yourself from more entities attaching to you and begin trying things out for yourself. I want to keep in touch with you and let me know your progress."

And that's how the session ended. I felt like I would explode. I went upstairs and found Tracey in our kitchen and didn't waste any time unraveling the entire story. She was stunned but happy that someone had finally helped me feel better. Because she had been through so many weird experiences herself she wasn't too shocked by some of the things the psychic had said. I felt like I had turned a major corner in my life.

Four days later, I had my appointment at the sound clinic. I almost called to cancel because I felt like the psychic had done so much healing that I might not need sound treatment, but for some reason I kept the appointment.

I met the woman who had helped me the last time and she took me to a soundproof room that had a recliner like you'd have in your living room. She asked me to sit down.

She told me to relax as she put a sensor on my finger to monitor my heart rate and oxygen intake. She also gave me a pair of headphones and asked me to listen to various sounds she played and comment on them.

"Tell me if you like them, if you're indifferent... whatever comes to mind," she said.

The sounds were very machine-like and sounded like something between helicopter blades flapping and some sort of machine whirring. They also reminded me of the "Hemi-Sync" sounds I purchased from the Monroe Institute years before. These CDs had a number of similar sounds mixed with subliminal suggestions to help you quit smoking, become a better public speaker, etc.

I mentioned this to her, and I was surprised to hear her say she was familiar with Hemi-Sync. I tested out the waters with her and mentioned that I had read Robert Monroe's books. Then I asked her how she knew about the Monroe Institute.

"What, were you trying to have out of body experiences?" I laughed.

"OOBE," she laughed back, which is the acronym for Out Of Body Experience. This single comment did something. And that's when everything changed.

At first, I thought it simply showed me that she knew more about this stuff than she was letting on, so I decided to tell her in detail what had happened to me with the psychic healer a few days before.

As I related my story, the temperature in the room began to rise, and I felt some sort of electrical change between the woman and me. Minutes before, I was looking at her as simply a healing practitioner, but now I saw her in a completely different light. It was like I had found a long-lost relative. From this point on, I will refer to her as Regina.

Regina mentioned to me that she had had an out of body experience before, and when I told her the really intense things that the psychic had told me about me being like one in ten people in the world and that I had special gifts, Regina confided something in me.

"Your higher self has been coming to me for several days… ever since your first visit here. It's like you've been desperately asking me to heal you," she said. "I didn't know how to tell you."

I was floored by this. Maybe this was really the female the tarot reader saw who would be instrumental in my healing. I didn't know what to think.

I looked at Regina and she was beaming at me. "I'm so excited for you that you've decided to live in your higher self."

CHAPTER 10:
NEW GIFTS

Regina created a collection of sounds she said would help me, and she put them all on a small sound player with a headphones attachment.

On my way out, she and I traded email addresses and agreed to keep in touch. It was so bizarre to me that in a matter of an hour and a half I had found a soul connection as well as someone who could help me down the path to healing. It felt like a major turning point in my life combined with the spiritual craziness that had also ensued with the psychic healer four days earlier. It was definitely more than a coincidence.

I began listening to the therapeutic sounds on the headphones and consulted with Regina on my progress. Nothing major happened right away. She suggested I meditate while listening to the sounds to see how that felt. She began nudging me to think "magically" and told me things she did on a daily basis — like putting her open palms over her food and blessing it with energy — sort of like a cross between Reiki and saying grace. She encouraged me to "play around" with my abilities, so I began by trying to visualize various people and their higher selves when I meditated.

Since my meditation was closely linked to when I listened to my sounds, I was meditating once a day at first and then after a few weeks I was doing it 2-3 times a day. It soon became easier to see people in my mind's eye or "go in," as Regina called it, but at this point I was simply observing and not interacting in any way.

Then one night, I fell asleep on our couch while watching a movie with Tracey. My legs were propped up on an ottoman, and I didn't move from the moment I fell asleep to the moment I woke up at 2 a.m. to go upstairs to bed. When I awoke, a quilt was over me and wrapped partially around one leg, and I thought, "That was nice of Tracey to cover me up," and I struggled to unwrap it and went upstairs.

Then, somewhere between 2:15 and 2:30 a.m. I began shivering in bed uncontrollably, and I woke up with a deep chill. I went to the closet, grabbed a T-shirt and a pair of sweat pants and fell back to sleep.

When we woke up the next morning, I asked Tracey if she had put the quilt on me, and she said she had not. In fact, the quilt had been folded behind my head and was partially stuffed behind the couch, she said. It would've been impossible for me to have accidentally moved it myself, especially considering the fact that I was in the exact same position the entire time. I immediately thought my angels had done it, and this struck me because in the past something like this would've raised goosebumps on my arms and probably freaked me out in a bad way.

But it didn't end there. I checked my email in the morning and noticed a message Regina had sent the night before. In it, she described working on and healing my astral body by putting me in a hot tub of liquid healing energy, surrounded by leagues of angels. Apparently, this was something she had been doing for a few days and she usually drifted off to sleep while I was still in there being cared for by my angels. But that night I got out of the tub and appeared to be shivering. Regina said she tried to wrap me in the warmest and softest cashmere blanket that she could imagine, and she left me there smiling as she finally did go to sleep.

This news completely blew me away. It was as if work Regina and the angels had done on the astral plane had manifested on the material. It was miraculous, and yet part of me wasn't surprised. It was more of a confirmation that these things are not only possible but can happen anytime and anyplace.

A few days later, Regina sent me this email:

"I took you on a journey with me during my meditation last night, into a pillar of power and light. It was fantastic. You've been doing so much healing in such a short period of time. You've been consistently receptive and willing. At this point I feel like I'm not really doing much to help you heal. I feel like I'm witnessing your emergence. You were offered a crown in my meditation. Please accept it whole-heartedly on all levels."

The next time I talked to her she vividly described a scene where angels had offered me a crown in an area that was covered with sand where a crowd of spirits and angels were in attendance. Regina felt like she had been invited to witness and was honored. I didn't know what to make of it.

I was still struggling to feel better physically, yet all of these amazing things were happening to me on the astral plane.

A few days later, Tracey called me at work complaining of PMS symptoms and a migraine headache. In November of the previous year, she had contracted a bad sinus infection that left her feeling dizzy for weeks after the infection subsided, and her doctors initially thought she had vertigo. But a neurologist diagnosed her as having migraines that appeared with extra intensity around the time of her period.

While I was talking to Tracey, I remembered Regina's encouragement to "play around" with my energy, and I told Tracey to sit tight and I'd try to send her something. I'd never tried anything like this before but for some strange reason I felt confident I could do something for her. I concentrated on sending healing energy to her head, but I guess I needed a little work on my aim because her hand started heating up. She excitedly exclaimed, "That was REAL. Oh, my god!"

As I was doing my daily meditations and going in, my astral vision began to get better. In the past while settling down to meditate, I had always tried to get my mind to stop thinking and didn't concentrate on anything visual that came up. But now, I was focusing on the visual aspects and letting my mind take me where it wanted. Consequently, sometimes I would see things that didn't make sense and would attribute it to my mind playing tricks on me only later realizing that something significant had been shown to me.

*   *   *   *

TUESDAY

It was the beginning of May of 2006, and I had been attacking Lyme disease for exactly a year. Physically I didn't feel any major improvement but spiritually and mentally I was in a completely different place. I had new tools to not only fight the illness but the illnesses and difficulties of other people. I was also filled with hope for the first time in several years. To underline the magical things going on with me, here is an account of what transpired one particularly exciting week in May.

One Tuesday morning I awoke from a vivid nightmare. I was on a farm in Kansas somewhere with my maternal uncle, and he told me he wanted to show me something in one of the barns on the property. I remember getting an immediate feeling of dread as we neared the building and I was picking up on the feeling coming from my uncle that he knew he was leading me to something unpleasant.

As soon as he opened the barn door, my maternal grandfather appeared… the one who had attached to me several years before. His head looked gigantic and grotesque. It was shiny and about 10 times the normal size of a human head. Shock and fear coursed through my body as I saw him. He began speaking to me, but I awoke up at that moment.

Once I was fully awake, I had the distinct feeling that my grandfather was back and possibly attached to me again. I went about my morning feeling slightly depressed and drained of hope.

When I got to work that day, I wasted no time calling Regina, and I told her about the dream and asked her to go in and see if my grandfather was actually attached to me. She said she would, and then she promised to call me back.

About an hour later, Regina called and in a very calm voice told me my worst fears. Yes, he was attached to me and she had actually interacted with him and received some information. For some reason, I wasn't afraid as she told me these things.

Apparently, my grandfather's soul and mine have experienced several lives together and in most of them, I have been the dominant figure. In this lifetime, I agreed to play a lesser role with him if he promised to show me love and compassion in his role as a grandfather. For some reason, he decided not to fulfill his end of the obligation and because he was jealous of my strength and power, he was currently trying to make me appear weak to others. He was thwarting many of my daily actions and bringing on many of the most insidious aspects of my Lyme symptoms — mental fog, difficulty in speaking, fear of being in front of people, and depression. This news sent a shiver of anger that ran up my spine like fire. My grandfather also referred to me as the red dragon and I wondered if this had some sort of connection to the comment he had made to the psychic years before about him being from the lizard side of the family. I wasn't sure.

Regina said that my grandfather was attached to me by two cords — one above my right eye and another on my back. I asked her if she could get him off of me, and surprisingly she said no. "You can do it yourself," she said. I didn't know what to say other than, "How?"

She explained the steps I needed to take after going in… amassing love energy around my heart chakra and reaching out to my grandfather with love. I also needed to imagine cutting the cords and then applying healing energy to the wounds their removal would create on my energetic body. I couldn't imagine actually doing this all by myself, but Regina would not change her mind.

I wasn't upset with her, but I was still wondering how effective I would be when I hung up the phone. I figured I would do it when I got home that night when I could completely concentrate on what I was doing. But that didn't happen.

Suddenly I felt as if someone was rattling my cage mentally. I felt dizzy, depressed and out of control, like I could lose my mind at any minute. I instinctively knew where this was coming from and realized I had to do something then and there... right in my office at work. My grandfather was provoking me.

I worked in a typical corporate "cube farm" but I had an actual office with a door that was on the perimeter of the office cubicles. While I could shut my door and try to meditate, I didn't want anyone knocking on my door or simply barging in if I was going to be doing anything out of the ordinary. I took a stroll to the water cooler to survey the area, and since things were pretty quiet, I figured I could give it a try. On my way back, I experienced more "cage rattling" and this rankled me and made me more determined at the same time.

I shut my door, and left the light on in case somebody might actually come in. How weird would it be for someone to see me in the dark in a semi-Lotus position meditating? I simply leaned back in my chair and put one hand over both eyes to keep the light from shining in, and within an instant, I was in.

And my grandfather was right there standing about 15 feet away. I unplugged the cord from my right eye, sending pink light out, and I felt a lot of heat on that side of my head. He sent me back something green and black that stuck to my legs like a gel. At first, I thought this was a gesture of love or reconciliation, but when I looked down and saw it massing around my feet, I knew it wasn't good.

I got a little pissed off and tried to push it away with energy, but it stuck to me, so I burnt it all with an explosive jet of bluish-white flame. Where this flame came from, I have no idea. It seemed to have been instinctively generated by me. I told him not to anger me and that I was capable of sending him off to oblivion. I sent him more love, and he sent me back something that looked like bubbles that flew at me and filled my face with heat.

I wasn't sure this was a good thing, so I pushed him and knocked him back with an energy burst. I saw him fly backwards violently but because I had forgotten to detach the cord from my back, he didn't move very far. He was flapping horizontally like a rag doll in a gale force wind. I felt bad about that, embraced him and gave him pure love from my heart. I told him that I had always loved him unconditionally and asked him to release any other ties he had to my family and to be on his way.

He did not respond in kind and seemed determined to stay, and this angered me even more. Suddenly I felt myself growing in height. I arose to be about 40 ft. tall and was very aware that I had taken on the form of a red dragon. I had not done this intentionally; it seemed like I was being guided somehow by my higher self. I was also on fire. I had immersed myself in the same bluish-white flame that had gotten rid of the green gel, and I suddenly wondered if my anger was turning me to evil. I didn't want to lose control over what I was doing!

After I cut the cord from my back, I turned to my grandfather and considered destroying his higher self, but I realized the finality of that. It's one thing to kill someone on the material plane, but there's something altogether different about destroying someone on the astral plane who isn't completely evil. I decided against it because it felt like it went against the laws of nature.

Instead, I yelled at my grandfather and told him never to cross my presence or that of any of my family members or I would destroy him, and then I cast him off into space.

I called upon angels to help heal me and regain my strength, and one came right to my side. I was aware of others around. I put up a force field and let the angels work on me. I summoned a pillar of golden energy from the heavens that filled the force field like water in a fish bowl.

And then I uncovered my face, opened my eyes and stepped back into the "real" world. I sat at my desk in silence for a while. Many thoughts were running through my mind. Had I just imagined that situation? Was I losing my mind? Did I suddenly have the ability to do astral warfare? What the hell was going on?

A few hours later, I contacted Regina and before I related my story to her, she told me what she had "seen," which was pretty much what I had also experienced. That amazed me that we could both go in at the same time and experience the same things. I had never heard of anyone doing this and it helped allay any doubt that my mind was playing tricks on me. I felt like I was moving into a new chapter in my life and that I might actually be able to do the things that Regina and a handful of psychics had told me I was capable of doing. It was a powerful gift that gave my life new meaning.

Later that night, I went home and told Tracey the whole story. I half expected her to question my sanity, but she didn't. She was happy that I had avoided harm and was supportive that I might be able to help others as well.

But I was still a little paranoid that my grandfather might come back, so later that night, I went back in to survey the situation.

I started off a bit ornery. The more I thought of my grandfather, the more indignant I got, and I was determined to wipe him off the face of the universe if I encountered him again. I went in with a chip on my shoulder and felt my anger transform me into a dragon and actually saw my dragon breath coming from me as I scanned the astral plane looking for him.

I eventually calmed down, and I started to work on a friend who had requested I do some energy balancing on him. I had unraveled the whole story about my newfound gifts to him the week before and he was overwhelmingly positive and supportive about it. In fact, he said he had been feeling "off" lately and asked if I could take a look at his astral body.

I found him on the astral plane, lying on the ground and twisted like an ant that had been stepped on. I blasted him with energy and love and he straightened out a bit. I wandered away from him and my heart began to hurt. I couldn't tell where the pain was coming from but realized it was my friend's depression. I embraced him and told him it would be OK. The heart pain seemed to subside when I did this.

Then I went a bit crazy. I started throwing astral fireworks all over the place. I summoned angels to work on my friend and it got very bright. I started throwing light and energy around like Roman candles from my hands.

I did this only for a second or two and it instantly occurred to me that this would attract the wrong kind of attention. Not a split second after this realization, a huge black thing came hurtling toward me with a head that was shaped roughly like a giant vampire bat, spanning about 8 feet in diameter. I blasted it very, very hard with white flame. It didn't go away at first, so I hit it again and again until it was gone.

Then things calmed down a bit and I set up a giant force field around me and stepped back into normal consciousness.

Shortly after, I sent an email to Regina describing the situation, and I received one from her at about the same time. In hers, she described watching me work on my friend and then suddenly throwing showers of sparks around. Her reaction was, "The crazy guy's got a gun! Everybody duck!" and she moved to the periphery to a safe place. As soon as she did, she saw the giant black thing coming toward me and tried to warn me. I never heard her, but she witnessed me simply turning to notice it and easily dispatching it with a flick of my finger. This differed from my own perception of having a bit of difficulty and needing to blast the thing several times. Still, I was amazed by the details she described without having yet read my email. When I called her on the phone the next day to talk about the incident, she still hadn't read it.

WEDNESDAY

I talked to Regina in the morning about what happened the night before, and then went about my normal work day. But a few hours later she called back sounding distressed. Apparently, her mother-in-law had called her to tell her of an alarming development with her nephew. He was nine years old at the time, and he woke up that morning speaking nonsense and laughing in a weird way. His behavior was completely out of character to the point of being alarming. Regina's mother-in-law was also sensitive to spiritual activity and things of the paranormal, so at one point she asked the nephew if there was someone else there with him, and he nodded his head. Regina also explained to me that her mother-in-law lived in an old farmhouse that was possibly haunted and that the room where her nephew was staying was sometimes cold and foreboding. Regina had sensed activity in the room before, and now she was afraid that some sort of spirit or entity had invaded her nephew's body. She stopped short of using the word "possessed."

Regina said that she had called me to help her get rid of this thing. I was shocked on several levels. How bizarre was it that this was happening not 24 hours after the incident with my grandfather? It was so hard to believe that I almost didn't believe Regina at first but listening to the concern in her voice let me know that all of this was very real.

The other issue was the fact that I felt like I had only just gotten my wings the day before and now I was being asked to fly across the Atlantic. Messing with demons or negative beings also completely creeped me out.

I told Regina I would think about it and try going in with her later that night, and she wasn't pleased. She ended up calling me back within the hour to say that her nephew was worse and that her mother-in-law was keeping him home from school. The issues needed to be addressed immediately. I had to help now, and I was still at work.

So, I agreed to do it, hung up the phone and did my stroll around the cube farm to make sure no one was around. I closed my door, sat down in my seat, and covered my eyes with one hand. Two minutes later, one of my employees called on the phone and I was ripped from my meditation. After dealing with the work issue, I went right back in.

I didn't see much at first, but sensed Regina's presence. Not long after, I felt activity from her and then got a feeling she was in trouble. This upset me and I "yelled" really loud to freak out whatever it was she was dealing with, and I think that rattled it loose.

I found a young boy lying on his back. His entire body was embedded in a black gelatinous substance with only his face exposed. His face seemed to have some sort of white powder on it. Seeing something so obviously evil engulfing a helpless little boy angered me, so I blasted around his body with positive energy. It was just an instinct, but I was guessing this energy force wouldn't harm non-evil things.

The black mass was removed, and I saw the boy as a cartoon caricature... sort of two-dimensional, like an anime/Japanese drawing. He had big eyes, brown hair and a green shirt and black shorts. He flitted around in the breeze like a two-dimensional piece of paper, and I got the impression that he was happy to be free. I embraced him and gave him love, and I turned to Regina to see how she was doing. I summoned golden light from the heavens that engulfed us all in a pillar.

Later on, Regina emailed me her account of what had happened and once again I was stunned by how similar it was to my own. I almost laughed out loud when I read the subject line before reading the actual email. It was addressed to: "Destroyer of Darkness."

According to Regina, she had gone in first, felt me for a while and then felt me slip away (because of my phone call). She saw that her nephew was encased in the same black substance that I saw, but she gave a much more detailed description of how it had infiltrated his body, was wound around his spine and had entered his brain. She felt me return, and because she is a healer and an empath, her first instinct was to jump inside her nephew's body in an effort to heal him from within. Unfortunately, as soon as she touched the black stuff, she was in trouble, and that's when I came to the rescue.

According to her, I appeared and simply destroyed the evil stuff with a wave of my hand. She did stay to work on her nephew for a while longer after I left.

I couldn't believe what I had just done, and it wasn't until later that I let myself grasp the full gravity of the situation. I knew that if I had allowed myself to be freaked out by an evil spirit possessing another body, I would have been gripped with the same kind of fear I experienced when watching the movie "The Exorcist" when I was a teenager. And if I were gripped by fear, I would be useless. Thankfully, my instincts had taken over, but now that it was all over, I was a little rattled by it.

But after processing it all, I realized that I didn't have anything to fear anymore. That didn't mean I could be careless, but now I knew I was capable of fending for myself, and if I ran into trouble, I had angels and other entities around me for protection.

THURSDAY

The next day Regina emailed me that her nephew was much better and actually went back to school. That surprised me in light of everything he'd been through. He had napped after we had worked on him and had headaches throughout the night, but the next day he was in good shape. She also said that her mother-in-law was concerned about the room where he was staying. In the middle of her saying prayers and using sage to clear the room, something "side-swiped" her in the head, so later on Regina helped her bless the room and seal it.

That night, I did something I had never considered trying before. After going in and working on a few friends of mine, it suddenly occurred to me that I could attempt to contact Jesus. Regina and a few other light workers I had talked to mentioned to me that they routinely summoned Jesus to help them do healing work and that he usually came. It blew my mind that he was always around and so available. I guess there was some sort of unspoken rule I had been taught in my Protestant upbringing that Jesus was only available through prayer and that it usually wasn't a two-way conversation unless you needed psychiatric help or were experiencing some sort of modern miracle.

So, I cast aside my old mindset, and felt I had the right to at least make an attempt to interact with him. One second after thinking this, I felt myself rise up from the area I usually inhabit when going in. I knew I was in his presence but could not see him. I asked if I could embrace him and everything went crazy. Energy was everywhere in every part of my being. It felt like I had been blasted into sub-atomic particles and that only my consciousness was there to pull me back together.

I said to him, "Guide and protect me and I will serve as

your instrument." And then I felt myself return to normal consciousness.

FRIDAY

The next morning, I did a bit of meditative traveling as I lay in bed waking up.

I went to my daughter Carly and actually saw her bouncing up and down like a little maniac. Not surprisingly, I tried to calm her down but was only partially successful. On a side note, when I later went downstairs to get her out of her crib, she had stripped down to her diaper and was actually bouncing up and down in her crib like a chimp. I had my shirt off when I picked her up, and this caused her to comment, "Daddy, I have little boobs and you and Mommy have big boobs!" As you can see, she was a piece of work at the age of two and a half.

Then I went to Jesus again in my meditation. I bowed on one knee and asked him to give me the eyes to see him.

I was completely overwhelmed by how he presented himself. I half expected him to materialize in a familiar form… robed, long hair and bearded, but instead he appeared in jaw-dropping immensity. He hovered over me like an aircraft carrier. His face filled the sky in my view and stretched the extent of my vision. I asked for guidance or a message and I immediately got one. My three roles to serve are as follows:

1. Healer
2. Warrior against the Dark
3. Teacher/Messenger

I also received a strong message about who he is. He is a soul like all of us who has been chosen to be a messenger as well, but he's incredibly huge and powerful — and has been around forever — like somewhere between an ancient non-human entity and an earthbound soul.

It felt like my life had entirely changed after everything that happened earlier in the week and I was feeling more confident than ever about my spiritual transformation. It was also amazing to me that anyone I told about my experiences completely accepted what I had to say and didn't question my sanity, at least not to my face. And in several cases as soon as friends found out about what I could do, they reflexively asked me to do work on them.

On Friday night, I agreed to work on a friend who had been struggling with some personal issues. We scheduled a time when she would be in a relaxed state and I would do the work. It ended up being around 10 p.m., and she later told me that she had been watching TV in bed with her cat when her cat suddenly jumped and acted as if someone had entered the room behind them. Apparently, the cat was feeling my energetic presence. She then said she felt heat wash over her as the session began.

I did a good bit of energy work on her and during the process, I took on some of her physical pain; my shoulder, back and stomach all erupted in paroxysms at the same time. I doubled over, and the angels came to heal me. After everything had been removed, I instinctively went to Jesus again.

This time something strange happened. I waited in his presence for some kind of message or communication, and then suddenly I saw a disembodied, outstretched arm that held a hooded black cloak. I was told to wear it whenever I went in.

The thing I thought strange about this was that on the other side, at least in my experience, the good guys come cloaked in white and shine bright light and the bad guys are surrounded by darkness and cold. In other words, the good guys wear white hats and the bag guys wear black hats. It's really that simple. So why was I given a black cloak?

Then I realized that this cloak was not only a means of protection, but it also doubled as camouflage for me. I had experienced troubles in the past for being a bright light that didn't protect itself, and sometimes brightness attracts bad things. This would conceal me while I did my work.

Things also changed for me in how I was going in. I used to depend on my therapeutic sounds to get me into a relaxed state so that I could enter the astral plane, but after my experiences in my office, I realized I didn't need them anymore. I also didn't need an extended warm-up process to get me in. Under certain circumstances, I could go in instantly without any kind of preparation.

I also listened to several other light workers' advice about protecting myself. I ended each session by surrounding myself with a golden egg of love energy that emanated from my heart. This created a force field of protection from the dark.

When going in, I was now putting on my crown, donning my cloak (which seems backwards), and putting on a golden armored breast plate that I made for myself after suffering a few attacks to my abdomen from entities that were attached to friends I had been working on. This routine came about instinctively, and I still do it today.

CHAPTER 11:
THINGS SHIFT

I continued to work on friends and relatives over the next two months, but I felt frustrated that the Lyme symptoms were not getting much better. I had an initial upsurge of energy after the bicillin injections stopped, and my doctor decided at that point that it might be wise to go off the antibiotics and watch the reaction.

Within a week I had more energy and was more lucid. I went back to the gym and started lifting weights again. I was also at the top of my game as far as spiritual pyrotechnics, so things seemed very hopeful for a while.

But I still couldn't shake the persistent fatigue that routinely hit me after every meal, and gradually this worsened by the end of the summer.

I felt like I was possibly slipping back, and I contacted the doctor's office and made another appointment.

One night as I slipped into bed with Tracey, something odd happened. She was lying with her back to me and as I lay down to spoon her, I closed my eyes and was immediately "in." I saw Tracey's body as it was positioned in bed, but she was lying on a hillside that overlooked a valley. It was night time and the sky was clear with a full moon. I noticed four to six shapes rotating in a circular motion above this valley. They looked like balloons with grotesque faces on them. They were black and stretched down almost to the ground from their height of about 20 feet or so, and their faces were gray. These faces looked similar to ancient, grotesque theatre masks, and their appearance was very creepy. Yet the overriding emotion I felt when looking at them was revulsion and anger. They made me want to kick their ass. They were obviously up to no good, so I quickly dispatched them with a blast of mental energy and then fell right to sleep.

The next morning Tracey began telling me of a dream she had had the night before. "I woke up and saw these ugly balloon faces right in our bedroom," she said. "Right over there" (she pointed to an area near our master bathroom).

I said, "Did you dream this, or did you actually see it?"

"Well, I was awake, I guess but I was so tired I thought I was dreaming. I closed my eyes and looked again, and they were still there but moving closer to the bed. I hated those things."

When I told Tracey what I had seen, we both felt our skin crawl. Those spirits had actually physically manifested in our bedroom. But because I had dispatched them, no harm had come to either of us. It let me know I couldn't let my guard down and I needed to continually protect myself, my family and our house.

* * * *

I made an appointment with the physician's assistant in the late summer and after hearing my complex array of symptoms and general tale of woe, she took another look at me and said, "You LOOK toxic." She gave me a round of tests that later showed that I had signs of a "co-infection." Another bacteria was present called *bartonella* along with a mild shadow of borrelia (Lyme bacteria). This explained why all of the traditional Lyme antibiotics hadn't been completely effective. I had apparently been fighting the battle on only one front while another entire army was going unchecked. I was prescribed Levaquin and felt my spirits lift. I saw an online video from well-known Lyme specialist, Dr. Joseph Burrascano that showed that many of his chronic Lyme patients had experienced complete recoveries after battling the disease for almost two decades by simply adding Levaquin to their regimens.

I stayed on oral Levaquin for about two months and noticed almost no difference. By the holidays I was back in my doctor's office. I had taken a new position at work that got me out of a bad situation with a hostile boss, but the new role was a step up in rank and much more demanding mentally.

One morning, during a meeting with the higher-level executives, I was asked to give a monthly review of my team. I was nervous going into the meeting but prior to me sitting down, I had a series of heart palpitations that triggered an episode of crippling brain fog. I could barely speak and as I began my presentation, I stumbled on a word I wanted to use. It was a simple word that I used every day, but it suddenly wasn't available to me. For some reason I began to panic. My brain shut down, my vision began to blank out and I started hyperventilating — right in front of everyone. I broke out in a sweat that soaked through my shirt back and armpits. Everyone stared at me and the department president saw me struggling and said, "Take a deep breath and start over."

I couldn't speak and my boss picked up where I had left off and I sat there silent, feeling like an idiot or mental invalid.

When the meeting ended, I retreated to my office and closed the door to regroup. My boss, who had been relatively hostile at that point, showed some signs of sympathy by coming to my office to ask what had happened.

"Was that the Lyme disease?" he asked.

When I replied that it was, he told me to take the rest of the day off. Many Lyme patients don't experience visible proof of impairment like this, and that leaves many observers to think a patient is really fine just because they don't look like they're actively dying.

This prompted me to make the appointment with my doctor, and he prescribed another brain scan. It was almost exactly a year to the day I had my last SPECT scan at Norwalk Hospital. The results showed that I had reduced the original problem area on my left lobe but now had a smaller area on my right lobe. Intravenous meds were prescribed. This meant getting another PICC line installed, and the news hit me like a jail sentence.

I first went on vacation to Florida with Tracey and Carly to visit Tracey's dad, and the day I returned, I took the train to Manhattan to get the line installed. This time it was done in the doctor's office by someone who knew what she was doing. A specialist threaded the line to its mark without the use of an X-ray and I had no problems with the line jabbing my heart. It was still no fun by any means. Having the line threaded took about twenty minutes and it was done with no anesthesia. It felt like someone jabbing a ball point pen into the crook of my elbow and then moving it around like someone working a manual gear shift on a car for twenty minutes straight. It wasn't agonizing, but it was painful and annoying.

I was given a cardboard box of meds and supplies — like bandages, alcohol wipes and extra tubes — and I made the lonely ride back on the train with the box under my arm. At one point I almost passed out on the train from the vasovagal reaction of having something invading my veins, but I managed to keep it together.

That first night I spiked a fever from the meds and stayed home from work the next day. The second battle had begun.

Dealing with the PICC line and the daily administration of antibiotics was no day at the beach. Each morning I'd wake up feeling just OK, and within about an hour the symptoms would start. By mid afternoon I would be so foggy and fatigued, I couldn't get through the day without some kind of help. I was prescribed Adderall, which is a brain stimulant used in hyperactive children as a substitute for Ritalin, and on most days, that was the only thing that kept me functioning. The problem was it also had side effects. I got massive headaches if I took it more than a few days in a row, and it is extremely habit forming. Luckily, that wasn't a problem for me.

I also needed to deal with the daily maintenance of the line and the meds. I kept pressurized plastic balls of antibiotics that the doctor's office shipped to me every week in my downstairs refrigerator (originally installed to store beer).

Each baseball-sized orb was connected to a plastic tube that ended in a nozzle that connected to the line installed in my arm. I had to warm up the meds so that they wouldn't go into my veins cold, and I usually did that by putting the ball in my pocket about 15 minutes before getting dosed. I had to find some place away from Carly to hang out while being "plugged in." I managed to do all of my infusions out of her sight except for one, and I hope that she soon forgot it. I usually just watched TV, read or worked on the computer, and I always got mentally fogged out at the end of the dose. I knew when my meds were gone when the ball had completely deflated. Almost every dose made me feel like crap.

On the weekends, a nurse would come to clean the dressing on my arm. The place where the line emerged looked brutalized, like I had suffered an arrow wound or something. It stayed slightly bloody almost the entire three months I had the line, and it was always tender to the touch. The nurse would have to delicately remove a large cellophane bandage that covered the entire area, and underneath was gauze that kept the line in place. All of this needed to be changed and she would swab the area with alcohol or betadine and spend a lot of attention to the open wound itself. This felt like having the line re-installed all over again for a few seconds; it was the same irritating and painful feeling. After it was all cleaned up and new bandages were applied, the nurse would draw blood to monitor my body's reaction to the meds.

To make things less convenient, I couldn't get the thing wet. I tried wrapping my entire arm in cellophane when taking a shower and attempted to hold it outside the curtain for most of the time, but that was futile. After getting it absolutely soaked a few times, the nurse told me about a rubber mitt I could order that went all the way up my arm and kept it so dry and air tight that I could actually swim in it. It looked like a lobster claw on one end and then turned into the arm of a wet suit. I had to slide this thing over my arm every time I showered, while being careful not to jab myself in the wound when doing so.

Dealing with all of this was demoralizing and it made me not want to leave the house unless I really had to.

One day in late January, I reached the point where I felt I might actually have a nervous breakdown.

A wave of frantic energy rushed through my brain and I simultaneously felt depression, anxiety and sadness one afternoon. I felt like it was someone or something rattling me from the "inside." I went to the privacy of my basement office where I usually meditate and went in immediately.

Seconds after going in I was shown some sort of vision that I didn't quite understand. I saw a figure cloaked in black who was given a crown and as soon as he was crowned, his body began radiating gold light. I wondered if this was me, but at points I seemed to be at this person's feet and saw he had a thin mustache. I wasn't sure what all of this meant. Soon I could feel myself going inside this person's body, and I later came to the conclusion that I was witnessing my own healing at the hands of "others."

Not long after this, I began to try to heal myself during meditation. I asked for help from the angels, and instantly I was flooded with intense heat that was concentrated on my face and neck.

I asked the angels to move around various parts of my body that needed healing and then I asked them to restore my confidence and resolve and to make my thoughts more lucid. Within minutes, I went from feeling almost suicidal and hopeless to feeling hope, happiness and love.

During this time, I began to get very confused about the conflicting experiences of having these fantastic gifts and being able to heal others while still suffering from my own maladies. I became very determined to heal myself, but each time I went in I was only able to make myself feel better for a limited amount of time. And eventually, I began to feel so bad that I wasn't mentally capable of going "in" very effectively.

Then other things started piling on. In February of 2007 (as was described in the introduction of this book), I was hit with a severe upper-respiratory infection that put me on my back for five days with a high fever. Less than 10 days later, I was leveled by an intestinal infection that left me feverish and on my back again. My immune system was obviously being compromised from the use of long-term antibiotics and I was directly hit by any germ my daughter brought home from pre-school.

While all of this was going on, a substitute nurse came to clean my PICC dressing and managed to damage the line which forced me to have it re-installed through surgery at the hospital. It was a rough stretch of time and it's what prompted me to begin writing my story.

I began to get back on my feet eventually but my communications with Regina dwindled and I spent much less time on the "other side." The sickness pulled me down, and when I did go in I concentrated on trying to work on myself. It wasn't very effective. Weeks before, Regina had recommended I try working on someone else and that might cause something to change. As it turns out, she was right.

I had not felt compelled to work on anyone in almost two months, but after a heated email exchange with one of my friends, something clicked. Out of the blue he had sent me some angry emails that were out of character for him but instead of reacting like most people would by returning his anger, I took a step back to consider the real source of his distress. I felt that he was actually reaching out to me for help, and when he sent a final email apologizing that he was feeling particularly edgy because it was the anniversary of his father's death, I knew I was right.

Years before, my friend's mother had died from failed surgery, and his family initiated a malpractice suit against the hospital and eventually settled out of court for a large sum of money. The combination of the financial windfall and loss of his mother sent him through a range of extreme emotions and just as he had begun to deal with it, his father died of heart problems a few years later. I was a pallbearer at both of their funerals and felt very close to his family.

I had told him about my experiences in recent months when he and his wife came to visit one weekend. In fact, he and I stayed up late one night and while talking about the subject of spirituality, I actually pushed love energy to him that heated up his body and he confirmed that he felt it.

So when I realized he was grieving and unconsciously reaching out to me for help, I decided to try to go in and work on him and possibly help him through his grief. I never thought about asking his permission because I felt that it was understood.

One morning before going to work and after Tracey and Carly had already gone, I tried working on him. When I went in, I was almost instantly "in" and he was there eagerly waiting for me. I first saw his eyes and focused on them for a while. Most of him was obscured initially (I could only really see him from his nose up), but I could tell he was thinner and appeared to me as a 17-year-old kid which was the age he was when we first met. He had a really short haircut, shaved all the way around with kind of a skullcap of hair on top. He was sad and anxious when I first encountered him.

I did a lot of deep-level work and balancing on him that ended with him winking at me and giving me the thumbs-up sign. This was a sign of approval and confirmation that the work was done.

As I began to move away from him, I was surprised that I hadn't seen anything or anyone around him, including both of his parents who had passed.

Not long after having this thought, I saw his mother. In the material world she was a very quiet and sweet, matronly woman who was very unassuming. At her funeral, the pastor's point of her eulogy was that women like her frequently go unnoticed in life, but they still can have a big impact on those around them. But on the other side of the veil she is an extremely bright light. She appeared to me as an angel, with only her face visible and beams of light radiating from it. She touched me with her love and warmth and let me know that she was grateful to me for taking care of her son and befriending her family. Her energy almost made me weep from the beauty of it. Still now, it's difficult for me to verbalize it without choking up. It felt like she had exposed me to the direct love and warmth from god. I instantly felt peace, warmth, ecstasy and love, and it was so powerful and positive that I did not like it when she disengaged from me. I then saw my friend's father standing next to her and he gave her a kiss on the cheek.

I got the information that my friend's mother and father had both provided for him by their passing. Because of his mother's malpractice settlement, my friend has been able to earn an engineering degree and provide for his own family. Their passing also provided a lesson for him that was intended to strengthen him, and it had been effective. Before his parents' passing, my friend hadn't had a care in the world and wasn't the most responsible person, but afterwards he matured and was supporting a family with a good job, and they had a nice place to live.

This event overwhelmed me in a good way and I actually went symptom free the entire day. I was so psyched about the experience that I couldn't wait to tell my friend about it, so I sent him an email right away. Because he was sensitive about talking about his mother's death, I wasn't sure how he would take the news I got about his mother practically sacrificing herself so that he could benefit from it. Still, I knew he would be happy to hear that both of his parents were watching over him.

But when I finally did talk to him, I learned a difficult lesson. My email to him had led him to be even more upset, and when I talked to him on the phone, he berated me for "trying to impose my beliefs" on him. I went from feeling very high about the experience to feeling devastated that I had crossed the line with him and hadn't asked for his permission to work on him. I was also shocked at his apparent change of heart from believing in the things I had talked about with him months before to him practically calling it quackery. The other confusing aspect was that his higher self had been so eager and grateful to me for doing the work on him.

After going back and forth for a while, I promised I would never work on him again or discuss this topic with him. But as we were ending the conversation, I mentioned halfway under my breath that I had seen his parents.

"But I guess you don't want to hear about it because you don't believe in it," I said.

"Well, you might as well tell me now," he said sheepishly.

I related the entire experience to him, and he was very happy to hear that his mother had transformed into an angel and that his father was nearby, and they were both watching over him. I braced myself for his reaction when I told him the message I had gotten about his parents sacrificing themselves so that he could prosper, and he said, "Oh yeah, didn't you ever think that?" I was so shocked I didn't know what to say other than, "NO!"

I didn't speak to him about this experience again for a year until he brought it up one day and told me that he was actually grateful to me for doing the work and finding out about his parents. He confided that he thought about it often and it made him feel good that his mother and father were aware of his new child and were looking over the whole family. I thanked him in turn for teaching me that I always need to ask permission before working on someone.

CHAPTER 12:
USING THE GIFTS

In the coming weeks, I began to feel better. I began going back to the gym and re-started my spiritual hygiene routines. It was late spring, and I felt that the higher air pressure and warmer weather was having a positive effect on me as well. I also started doing more energy work on family, friends and referrals.

About this time, a friend of mine reached out to me at work. Because of the nature of what I was doing, I didn't exactly go around telling a lot of people about my energy work but if the subject came up and the person in question responded to a few key phrases in the right way, I would open up.

My friend called me to tell me his mother was dying. He was very close with her and was very upset about it. She had lung cancer, which was actually her worst nightmare; yet she had been a smoker most of her life. I realized how her thoughts and intentions had possibly manifested this all to make her worst nightmare come true. The cancer had begun to move around her body and had lodged in her brain, causing some sort of stroke that put her in a coma.

I told my friend this sounded serious and that I didn't know how much I could do, but I promised to do everything I could. I had learned at this point that it was important for people to know that the work wouldn't always bring about the expected or desired result… but it would always help bring about the one god had in mind. I had also learned not to become attached to the end result. Getting a big head about doing great things was one thing, but it was also important not to get down when it seemed like things didn't work, and this next situation is a good example of that.

He told me that she was in a hospital overseas and that he hoped she wouldn't die before he got there. I told him that I would try to keep her alive until his flight arrived, and I asked if he could send a photo of her to help me do the work.

At my first opportunity, I went in when I got home and tried to visualize my friend's mother. He hadn't had a chance to send the picture, but I didn't let that stop me. I watched a woman appear in robes, and I did a good deal of energy work on her, opening up her chakras and clearing out impediments and densities I found around her body.

At the end of the session I saw her lie down and her robes went limp. I looked closer to see that her body had disappeared, but the robes remained. I didn't think that was a healthy sign.

I didn't hear from my friend for several weeks, so I didn't know the outcome for a while. I felt like I hadn't done that much, and I felt somewhat ineffective.

One afternoon while at work, probably a month after my friend first called me, I got another call from him. This time he sounded happier and he invited me to lunch. He said he had some things to tell me.

After sitting down and exchanging some small talk, I asked him how his mother was.

"She's better," he said, and I was surprised by what he told me next.

He said that she had awakened from her coma about twenty minutes before he made it to the hospital and the doctors were baffled as to what made her rise. They were expecting her to die. My friend actually mentioned to them that he thought I had had something to do with it. He didn't tell me their reaction, but I would've loved to have seen it.

He also told me that while her cancer had progressed, she was leaving the hospital to go spend time in an apartment he owned in the mountains. He was very grateful to me for helping his mother recover from the coma right before he got there because he was able to spend a lot of quality time with her during his visit.

I continued to work on her from time to time and during one of my sessions, I was pushed aside by a tall, dark figure. This man began to work on my friend's mother in a very dramatic way… by reaching his arm all the way down his mother's throat past his bicep and pulling out black material. I stood by and watched and then embraced her with positive energy and love when it was finished.

My friend's mother eventually succumbed to the cancer several weeks later, but he was able to spend valuable time with her in his apartment in the mountains before she passed away.

*   *   *   *

One early morning as we were getting ready for work, Tracey got a call from her friend Roseann. A close friend of Roseann's had undergone a bone marrow transplant and had been in and out of the hospital with heart problems in recent months, and now she was back in the hospital in a coma. Roseann called to see if there was anything I could do.

At this point, I hadn't worked on many people I hadn't actually met in person, so I asked Roseann if she could at least send me a picture of her friend. I waited a few hours and after not getting the picture, I decided to go in and look for her friend without knowing exactly what she looked like.

I waited until Tracey took Carly to pre-school and as soon as it was quiet, I went in. I started by calling Roseann's friend's name several times and I began seeing a woman materialize before me.

A woman's face came into view with sandy colored hair that was long and straight, and she was a bit overweight. I wasn't sure if this is what she actually looked like, but that image helped me zero in on her. I could only see her face at first, and she seemed to be submerged in water up to her neck. I tried very hard to drain the water or move it down so that she wasn't in danger of drowning, but whenever I did, she actually tried to push her own head under water.

After doing this for several minutes, I put her on her back and created a kind of giant life preserver for her that had flotation devices on either side of her. She still tried to duck her head under water backwards, and the more I tried to help her, the more I realized I was working against her wishes and that she wanted to die. So, I stopped.

Then suddenly I saw Ro's face. Her astral self was hanging out nearby. I did some minor work on her, and I saw her get upset and look in her friend's direction and start to yell at her. "Wake up, wake up! Wake the fuck up!" is what she was imploring. I tried to calm her down as she kicked and stomped her feet in frustration.

I gave her friend one more blast of energy and let her be.

I emailed the results of the session to Tracey and drove to work. When I got home that night, Tracey was waiting for me in the kitchen with a funny look on her face.

"Did Ro tell you anything about her friend before you worked on her?"

"No," I said. "I never even got a picture from her. Why?"

"Well, everything you said in the email happened."

I asked Tracey what she meant, and she explained that when Ro's friend was admitted to the hospital, she was experiencing heart problems, so the doctors flooded her heart with a fluid that accidentally backed up into her lungs. This is what caused her to go into a coma. The whole thing about drowning and her trying to drown herself rang true because Rosann told us that not only had the fluid literally caused her friend to drown but she had confided to Ro that she wanted to die.

Then Tracey also said that Roseann had been in the hospital alone with her friend the night before. After everyone had left the room, Roseann started yelling at her to wake up. I also seemed to have pretty accurately visualized what her friend looked like based on my description in the email.

The hair stood up on my arms and now I was surprised.

"How did you know all that?" Tracey asked.

"I don't know," I said. "I just SAW it!"

I knew it was wrong for me to get attached to the outcome of my work, but this news flooded me with a mixture of very good feelings. I nearly wept when Tracey told me all of this. I'd been weakened for so long. I was ready to explode with new energy!

*   *   *   *

Several weeks later, a friend of mine flew in from Texas to work on a music and recording project with me. He was well aware of the things I was doing, and on the day of his arrival he asked if I could perform Reiki on him.

So, a few hours after picking him up at the airport, I asked him to lie on his back on the carpeted floor of our den and I began his Reiki session. When I asked him to turn over on his stomach so that I could work on the other side of his body, I had the thought of trying to connect with his higher self while applying healing energy to his physical body. At this point, I had never heard of anyone doing this combination of things, but it seemed like a very natural thing to do.

When I made it down to a chakra in the middle of his back, I noticed an attachment he had. A bald child, probably 8-10 years old or so appeared. I was a little rough with this person at first because I thought it might be an evil entity, but when I pushed the person away, it snapped right back in place as if attached to my friend by a rubber band. This was when I realized it was a human spirit who had attached to him by a cord.

I mentally cut the cord and asked the person to leave, saying that it was OK to pass into the light and to move on with love. The child disappeared with no incident.

When the session was over, I remembered that my friend had once worked in a children's hospital.

"Did you ever have anyone die on you?" I asked.

"Yeah, all the time," he said, and he let me know it was a pediatric surgical unit and it was a very sad place to work. That's why he eventually transferred from that unit to a different hospital where he began assisting in childbirths.

I asked him if he had ever made a connection with a particular child, and he said that a strange thing had happened to him with one of his patients. He had made a strong connection with a girl who was dying of cancer and he had also connected well with her mother. Sadly, the girl eventually died but years after he transferred to the new hospital, a woman who was about to give birth recognized him as he was preparing her for delivery.

She revealed that she was the mother of the young cancer victim and now she tearfully told him he would be helping her bring a child into the world after helping her usher one out of it. I knew that this was the young girl who had been attached to him and to say that we were both moved by the realization doesn't even begin to describe it. To date, it's difficult for me to verbally recount this story without breaking down in tears because of how many emotions it brings up in me.

*   *   *   *

During this time, Carly's verbal skills emerged and we became more and more amused by her previously-suppressed thoughts. One thing that was revealed was her fascination with her great grandmother Lola. Carly never met her because she passed about six years before Carly was born, but that didn't stop her from asking us questions like, "When Lola takes a nap in heaven, are there comfortable beds?"

One day she declared, "Lola's dead… not the kind when alligators pull you into the water dead, but the kind-in-heaven dead."

But the comment that stunned Tracey and me was what Carly told us when she was only about two years old. Carly had suffered a complicated birth with her being strangled by the umbilical cord, having meconium expelled in the womb and getting stuck in the birth canal (which was mentioned in detail in Chapter 5). She got to a point to where she had advanced too far down the birth canal to have a C-section performed. She was stuck, her heart rate was dropping, and it became a lift-threatening situation for both her and her mother. Tracey didn't have any strength left but she suddenly gained the energy for one final push and felt the gentle presence of Lola in the room. I had felt her presence as well, and Tracey and I both sensed that Lola had helped with that final push to bring Carly into the world. But we never mentioned anything to Carly about it.

One day Tracey and Carly were talking about Lola and Tracey began to sob. When Carly asked why, Tracey told her that she sometimes cries when thinking of Lola because she misses her. Carly replied, "I know, Mama, I cried for Lola, too. I saw Lola when I was trying so hard to come out of your belly. Don't you remember?!"

Tracey was speechless. We took this as Carly's confirmation that Lola had had a hand in aiding her birth and this was her version of the story.

This prompted us to ask Carly if she had ever seen Lola outside of that situation. She replied, "No, except that one time when I was really little and had small feet like someone shrunk them and I was in my carriage. Lola was smiling at me." Again, we were floored. First of all, the word "carriage" was a term Lola had used and we never did, and the comment about her looking down at her own tiny feet gave us a really cool view into her perspective.

It also showed us that she had an outrageous memory. Later that year, Carly had some skin eruptions that looked close enough to the erythema migrans or bull's eye rash you get with a tick bite that we took the precaution of having her tested for Lyme. Thankfully, the test came back negative, but we went the extra mile and paid for a special test that had to be administered at Norwalk Hospital. It was Carly's first time back there since her birth and NIC unit ordeal. While Tracey and Carly were walking hand-in-hand through the halls, Carly ran over to one of the walls, patted it and said to Tracey, "This is where I'm from." Tracey and I still can't believe she said that.

CHAPTER 13:
ANOTHER SHIFT

After the second PICC insertion and extraction, I felt almost back to normal for about three months and then I began to experience brain fog and other symptoms again. My Lyme doctor noticed this and remarked that he had seen patients like me have symptoms disappear for about three months after a round with PICC meds. This was because bacteria was being cleared out in the blood stream, but it was migrating outside of the circulatory system and going dormant while the meds were present. He also suggested testing me for *babesia*, which is a parasite that commonly tags along with other tick-borne bacteria. I tested positive and he put me on a few rounds of Mepron, which is a very expensive anti-malaria drug. A bottle of a monthly supply cost me $400 even after insurance coverage.

At the same time, I was taking three different oral antibiotics and I began to slip back into the familiar cycle of symptoms and depression. One night while playing in a band in Austin, TX, I almost passed out on stage but soldiered through my performance in a trance-like state. I had no idea what was going on with me and I decided it was a sign that it was time to switch doctors and protocols.

I learned about another Lyme-literate doctor in Manhattan, NY who primarily prescribed herbs and Chinese remedies. He was not averse to using these meds in tandem with antibiotics which I did for a time. The herbal meds he prescribed seemed even more powerful than the antibiotics and I had dramatic herx reactions — openly sweating, having to take naps during the day and feeling loopy without warning.

At one point I was taking pills of *allicin*, a natural antibiotic derived from garlic. They made me radiate the smell of garlic out of every pore in my body. After taking them for only a day, a coworker walked a few steps into my office at work and said, "Why does it smell like a pizza parlor in here?"

It traveled with me in a cloud and became a source of embarrassment and open jokes during meetings at work. The pills were also so powerful that I couldn't tolerate them for more than a few months. They leveled me with herxes and side effects until I couldn't take it anymore. I had a phone consult with the doctor and he suggested dialing back my dosages and replacing allicin with a different herb.

I began to feel better after a time, but later that winter I developed a deep lung infection that turned into walking pneumonia. It took me three months to shake it and it showed me how compromised my immune system had become from being on antibiotics for multiple years.

In December, I went to a new general practitioner who prescribed more antibiotics in addition to what I was already taking. When I came back two weeks later, he looked a little worried and prescribed a chest X-ray for me while he was writing a prescription for a different antibiotic.

"Why the chest X-ray?" I asked.

"To see if you have pneumonia," he said.

"So, if you found out I have pneumonia, what would you do?"

"Prescribe the antibiotics I'm prescribing right now…"

After hearing that, I thought I'd give my body a break and not subject it to any more radiation… so I didn't go get the X-ray.

Two weeks later, I was back again, and he was a little miffed that I hadn't gotten the X-ray, but he prescribed a third antibiotic.

"We're running out of ideas," he said.

I made a half-hearted joke to him that it seemed impossible for any germ to be getting through the line of defense I had going with more than three antibiotics, but he didn't think it was that funny. That's when I realized the antibiotics were more than likely causing the problem by tearing down my immune system and actually making me more susceptible to bacterial invasion. I decided it might be a better idea to go off of all antibiotics all together, which was pretty counter intuitive, considering how sick I was.

And oddly enough, being on the antibiotics had been a source of security since they made me feel I was actively fighting the illness with them. But when I thought back to my time on them, they had been the most symptom-filled, depressing years of my life. Could it be any worse if I went off of them and stayed on the herbal treatments? I figured I could always return to them if I wanted, but the more I read about how harmful long-term use of antibiotics are to your gut, immune system and even DNA, I knew I would be better off without them.

Within a month and a half of discontinuing the synthetic meds, I began to feel a lift and noticed the random incidences of brain fog that had dogged me on antibiotics were much less frequent. I also learned more about the importance of detoxing while building up my immune system so it could do more of the work without depending on pharmaceuticals.

I was feeling better than I had in years, but I was nowhere near feeling back to normal. I've found that Lyme patients tend to rate their level of health and wellness by percentages and I had instinctively done this when visiting doctors over the years. While I was on antibiotics I was at 35% optimal health and now I was somewhere in the 65% range. I still had a way to go, but I had gone through every known treatment for Lyme that I had access to or knowledge of. I seemed to have reached the final plateau.

*   *   *   *

In late April, my parents came to visit us for a week. Everyone was happy and healthy, relatively speaking, and it was a good visit overall. On the morning they left, Carly, Tracey and I all waved goodbye to them in the driveway. A few hours later all hell broke loose. I started experiencing old Lyme-like symptoms and Tracey started getting severe abdominal pain.

Later in the afternoon, I took some of my old antibiotics and went upstairs to lie down for an hour while Carly took a nap. Twenty minutes later, Tracey woke me up to tell me we needed to go to the hospital. Pain from an ovarian cyst had erupted so fast and hard that she had already called her doctor, and he told her to go to the emergency room.

We woke up Carly, took her to my mother-in-law's house and went to the hospital. What a chaotic scene. They had a full house of patients, so it was a good hour before we even saw a triage specialist. They did a CAT scan and then sent us to a room where we waited another hour. Tracey's pain increased, so I closed the curtains and did modified Reiki on her. I concentrated on a dense area around her right fallopian tube where I sensed an ovarian cyst. I visualized breaking it up and giving it good energy, but the pain kept coming for a while.

Finally, we saw a doctor who said it didn't seem like a cyst but more like a kidney stone, and I began to question my intuition and abilities. First rule of healing: Don't get attached to the outcome of your healing!

When the doctors returned, they decided Tracey needed a sonogram to make sure the cyst wasn't restricting blood flow to her fallopian tubes. They wheeled her into the room for the scan and then she and I waited in a private waiting room for the results.

The look on the doctors' faces were priceless when they returned with the results.

"That's weird," one of the specialists said to us. "The cyst has started to collapse and it's already half the size it was an hour ago. We've never seen anything like this."

Tracey and I knew exactly what was happening and realized this whole experience was fast becoming a waste of our time. I could've just gone in and scanned Tracey at home and applied Reiki to heal her.

After spending seven hours there, we left and Tracey was doing much better. She stayed home from work the next day, but she was back to her normal routine the following day.

CHAPTER 14:
BLAST FROM THE PAST

One afternoon in April of 2010, I did my usual meditation and came upon something very interesting.

I was working on myself, releasing attachments and healing the areas of attachments. I found two, and after spending several minutes dispersing them, I saw a figure appear as the dust settled.

A very distinct image of a young female emerged from the disintegrating forms. It looked like a 9-year-old girl in sepia tone who was frantically beckoning me to follow her.

I decided I would and we immediately shifted into what looked like a turn-of-the-century city. Everything appeared black and white. She was hastily trying to lead me somewhere. I sensed that someone had been hurt or needed saving.

We turned a corner and she pointed at something and as I turned my gaze to my right to follow her finger, I realized where we were. We were near Île de la Cité in the center of

Paris during some kind of flood. I realized this girl was my sister from a past life and as I looked to the banks of the swollen Seine, I saw the horrified faces of gendarmes and rescue workers. They had found someone. I couldn't see who it was. Someone had drowned. And the detail of the gendarmes' hats and faces passed very near my gaze and then away.

I didn't know what to do. I couldn't see anything but the close-up faces of people in modes of panic, and I began to pull back and my consciousness rose above the activity. Then suddenly the scene shifted, and I saw a woman very distinctly, but she wasn't at the area of the flooding. I was seeing her in a happier time, in a living room or parlor. She had her hair parted in the middle and pulled tightly around her head in thin braids. She was matronly and plump, and she had her arms bent in front of her like she was hugging someone. She was singing a children's song, smiling and swaying from side to side.

Unconditional love poured out of me and I realized this woman was my mother. Mind you, this was not my mother in this lifetime. In fact, I didn't immediately recognize her as any relation of mine until I got an overpowering feeling and a message that she was my mother from the early 1900s. I felt very sad at her loss and began to sob when I realized she was the person who had drowned.

I was getting ready to go to work that day, but I couldn't keep myself from looking up photos from a flood in Paris. It didn't seem likely, but in no time, I found several photos of a rare Paris flood in 1910. Looking at the pictures, especially ones of the Seine overflowing to the top of its bridges like Pont Neuf, made me sob uncontrollably for some reason. I was feeling a very distinct loss of this woman and mother figure from 100 years before.

The next day I meditated to try to make sense of what I had seen, and I actually got more information and picked things up where they had left off. I sensed that my mother had beaten me fairly regularly and rather violently, which was not unusual for that time period. Yet, I knew she loved me and I definitely felt unconditional love for her. I tried to understand more information about the young girl who seemed to be my sister, but nothing came up. At one point, I saw myself as a young man and saw the woman whom I would marry in that time. To my complete shock, this woman looked very much like my mother today. At the end of this session, I began crying again, feeling the loss of my mother from so long ago.

On the third day, I went back into meditation to try to draw some kind of conclusion and closure to the situation. Why was I seeing these things now? I waited for a while but saw nothing. Then I felt the sudden compulsion to forgive my mother of this time for all the beatings she had given me. Within seconds of me doing this I saw myself and my 1900s mother above the Earth as if in outer space. Just as I had forgiven her, I received the knowledge that she had waited all these years for me to do so before taking on a new life in another body. The moment I forgave her, I watched her image stretch and spiral down to Earth as she began her reincarnation process. I was floored with this knowledge and knew that no amount of imaginings on my part could have concocted such an elaborate story so spontaneously. I had felt like a spectator through most of it, and now I felt like my forgiveness had provided some sort of healing across the expanse of time for my mother. The sight of photographs from this time and the thought of my mother no longer brought me to tears. Instead, it brings me happiness that I was able to help her release some sort of karmic debt to advance her spiritual growth. I also noted that the Paris flood of 1910 began on January 21 of that year and that my meditation occurred almost exactly 100 years later, give or take a month or two.

About a month later during my daily meditation, I felt the need to gain more answers. What is the nature of the universe? What's the answer to how things really are? As I was in deep meditation, I asked to be shown the "face of God" and to understand our relationship.

Within a second of thinking/asking this I saw a very large star/sun with tendrils that reached down to the Earth. I understood that the sun image was god and that these tendrils were connected to each of us and that information passes through them. The information goes both ways and it is how god stays in contact with us and is aware of our experiences while also pushing information downstream to each of us. My overall impression was that god is not in human form but is an expanse of limitless, creative energy and this energy masses together very much like a brain. We on the material plane and other beings across the dimensions and universe are connected to god and each other like a nervous system.

I snapped out of my meditation upon receiving this information. Again, no amount of my imaginings could have invented this, and I knew in my heart that the information was accurate.

Several months later, I was watching a television show that profiled the Egyptian pharaoh Akhenaten. He set himself apart from the other pharaohs and broke from religious tradition by putting forth the idea that there was only one god. Prior to this, the Egyptians had worshiped many gods at once, but during Akhenaten's reign, he focused on a single, all-powerful god named Aten. The symbolic representation for this god was a sun disk with tendril-like arms that reached down to the earth. I almost fell out of my chair when I saw the image. It was a crude but very similar representation of what I had seen during my meditation. This was too close to be some kind of coincidence.

CHAPTER 15:
HEALING MIRACLES

In the winter of 2010, I came across an online video of Oprah Winfrey profiling a healer in Brazil named John of God. For some reason I watched it, expecting it to be a video revealing the faith healer's abilities to be a hoax. Instead, I became transfixed by what I saw. A Harvard-trained doctor went to Brazil to debunk John of God's healings but could not. The Brazilian was healing thousands of people at a time without touching them, while also picking people from the audience to perform more sensational physical surgeries onstage. The patients did not flinch or bleed very much when he cut into them with a standard scalpel, and he didn't use sterile equipment or anesthesia. In some cases, he actually scraped the corneas of patients' eyes and they didn't recoil in pain. This seemed impossible to fake and yet the Harvard doctor remained skeptical even though he admitted he couldn't explain what he was witnessing.

On his final day there he mentioned something about understanding what he had witnessed in his head but not accepting it in his heart. As he was walking and talking with someone on camera after saying this, people in his group noticed a small amount of blood staining his shirt in the area of his heart. When he lifted his shirt, there was a tiny hole that was the source of the bleeding and it would not stop for over an hour. Someone off camera said he had just had a "psychic" or "invisible" surgery like many of the visitors who go to the see John of God, and this had "opened his heart." The look of bewilderment on the doctor's face said it all to me. This had not been a prank or hoax. Powerful healing of a totally different nature seemed to be happening in Brazil and I was intrigued.

A few weeks later, I felt at a crossroads in my life once again and felt the need to seek the advice of the psychic who had done the original remote releasement on me years before. I made a list of things to discuss and the final bullet on my list was "John of God."

At the end of our discussion, I asked her about him and I was surprised to find out she was very familiar with him. In fact, she was friends with a woman who ran tours to the "Casa" where John of God practices and she could put me in touch with her. Further, the tarot cards she read suggested I should go as soon as possible.

I felt compelled to act on this, but I also had reservations about leaving my family and going to a foreign country by myself on a 10-hour plane ride. After contacting the tour group, they highly recommended I spend two full weeks in a town very far off the beaten path named Abadiânia. None of this seemed likely or even possible for me to do. I mentioned this to the tour leader and she said that once I made the decision to go, I'd be surprised at how the universe opens up to allow it to happen.

And that's almost exactly what happened. In a few days after making a firm decision to go, I was able to take time off of work, obtain a visa, book my plane flight, and make arrangements with my family to be away for this extended time. I felt waves of guilt leaving Tracey alone with Carly in a single-parent situation for so long, but I also felt I was at the end of my rope in terms of options to complete healing. I had to do this, and I would see it through.

On March 12, 2011 I boarded a flight at John F. Kennedy Airport that stopped in Atlanta where I was to meet the other members of my tour group before we all boarded a flight to Brasilia, Brazil.

It was a group of about 25 people arriving from all parts of the U.S. and Canada. They were all above the age of 45, and all of them were women except for three men in their 60s. I was the odd man out. I was to later learn that all of the men in my group were there to support their wives and I was the only male visiting exclusively for a healing.

The tour leaders gave us some necklaces to wear and then went over some of the rules. During our days visiting the Casa, we needed to wear all white, including shoes, underwear, etc. If we had a "spiritual surgery," which was almost inevitable, we needed to follow a special diet and take specially-prepared pills that were infused with energy and made from a harmless passion flower (passiflora). Some of the rules seemed strange and almost cultish and others seemed third world... like the fact that we couldn't flush toilet paper down the toilets and instead needed to put it in a waste basket in our bathrooms. There was limited phone and internet service and we were told this was a good thing to enable us to disconnect from the life that had undoubtedly contributed to any illness or issues.

I had no idea what to expect. I knew I would follow all of the protocols, but I didn't fixate on them. Some in the group did and were concerned they would "screw it up" or ruin their healing experience. The group leaders tried to reassure everyone that everything was happening in divine order and that the minor miracle of simply coming to Brazil would unfold into a larger one.

Due to the stress of travel, some Lyme symptoms had emerged, and I felt fatigued and foggy on the flight. I scanned the plane and thought I could recognize other visitors of the Casa outside our group. Many were wearing saris and tunics, mostly in white, and they had that unmistakable look of hope on their faces.

I slept fitfully through the night and awoke as the rays of dawn poked through the clouds and into the window beside my seat. I stretched and said good morning to a woman sitting next to me who was wearing a sari and had the general look of a world traveler. Not surprisingly, she confessed that she was going to the Casa for the first time after having just spent five months in India on a spiritual pilgrimage. She was not visiting the Casa for healing purposes. She was leading a small group of pilgrims who needed to be healed, and she was going for her own spiritual reasons. This was the first time I had heard of anyone going to see John of God for a purpose other than physical healing, and it piqued my curiosity.

The woman saw the small travel guitar I had brought with me and said that she was also a guitar player and that maybe we could play some songs together if we found time in Abadiânia. I told her that sounded great, but I didn't expect that we would bump into each other randomly in town. She laughed and told me the town was so small it would almost be impossible for us *not* to bump into each other.

We said good luck to each other, disembarked from the plane, and I fell in with my group of pilgrims in the main arrival area of the Brasilia airport. After we had all gathered our luggage, a handful of shuttle vans picked us up to take us for the hour and a half ride to the town of Abadiânia.

The shuttle ride gave us all more time to get acquainted and share stories of healing, philosophies, etc. Many in our group readily revealed their purpose for visiting the Casa while a handful kept that secret. Almost all of the women in the group had some form of cancer and a few were in Stage 4 development. They admitted that their doctors had given up on them and told them to get their effects in order; there was nothing more that could be done. Yet these women bravely laughed that they were going to defy the odds with their visit to Brazil.

By the end of the ride, I was ready to find my room, and more importantly, my bed. I was jet lagged, which amplified other symptoms I was already experiencing. I stepped out of the van into the blazing Brazilian sun, which felt extra good because I had left snow on the ground in Connecticut. Here, it was a balmy 85 degrees with plenty of humidity.

As I waited for the others to depart from the shuttle, I spotted a beautiful flowering shrub next to the entrance of our hotel, so I snapped a few shots of myself by it. I didn't realize I was shooting my "before" photo that I would later use as evidence to show how sick, swollen, and unhealthy-looking I had appeared prior to seeing John of God.

The leaders of our tour group had wisely planned nothing for us to do on our arrival day other than getting acclimated to our surroundings or scheduling a therapeutic massage. While they encouraged us to wander around the small-town center of Abadiânia and go visit the grounds of the Casa, they warned against straying outside a certain perimeter that was not protected by the entities that worked with John of God. You could visibly see the line of demarcation. Inside the protected area was a quaint town where villagers drove horse-drawn carts, and locals sold crystals and souvenirs in small, but well-kept shops and restaurants. Outside the area looked noticeably run-down and was dotted with a few places that sold alcohol and played music at an edgy volume.

This was my first time in Brazil and my only knowledge of it was distorted by two movies I had recently seen... "City of God" and "Turistas" so I didn't have to be reminded to stay in our designated areas.

One thing the tour leaders did require was for us to each meet with them in a private counseling session before our group dinner that night. The purpose was two-fold: To help us focus on our healing intentions and to write a note that would be walked through the line and read by an interpreter as we met John of God.

I sat down with our tour leaders and they asked me why I had come to Brazil.

"To be completely healed of Lyme disease," I said, and I expected our little session would end right there and that they would give me some further instructions regarding our group meeting with John of God the next day.

Instead, one of them looked up from her writing and said, "And what else?"

I laughed and said, "What, do I get three wishes?" but my laugh caught in my throat when I saw the serious looks on the counselors' faces.

"Why stop at three?" smiled the other tour leader.

I loved this way of thinking and it immediately changed my attitude. I had seen videos of the powerful healing miracles John of God was bringing about and I also knew that not everyone needed visible and physical healing. Why limit the possibilities here?

I rattled off a few things but focused on one "wish" in particular. "I'm a musician, so I'd like to heal people with the music I write and perform."

And so it was done. The leaders handed me my note, gave me a few instructions about what would happen the next day and sent me on my way.

Our entire group met for dinner later that night in a large patio dining area and the buffet they served was spectacular. We all had huge appetites that night and every other night we gathered for meals. Everyone remarked that there was something about the energy of the place that made us eat ravenously. Even the smallest, slightest woman in her 80s was knocking back heaping platefuls of food that rivaled my own.

After dinner, we were instructed on the many rules of the Casa, foremost of which was the wearing of all-white clothing down to underwear and shoes. It was explained that the entities who would be bringing about our healing had a much easier time seeing our energetic bodies if we wore all white. There was also a rigid time schedule and we were instructed on where to stand in line. We were warned that busloads from all parts of Brazil would be arriving, and by 7 a.m. there would be thousands of people lining up for healing. We were given nametags with the name of our hotel and tour group to help identify us, and many in our group began to pepper our leaders with questions. The excitement of what was at hand had raised some nervous energy and many in our group didn't want to do something wrong after having traveled so far for a healing.

All questions and fears were laid to rest and we all turned in early that night, knowing that there would be a knock on our door at 6 a.m. from our tour leaders.

The knock came quicker than expected. I slept well that night and had to drag myself out of bed after giving an unintelligible yelp that I had heard the knock and would meet the rest of our group in the hotel lobby.

Everyone in our group was neatly dressed in all white, including our leaders, and everyone had a smile on their face belying nervous tension. Our leaders gathered us outside the hotel and there was a cool mist in the streets that spanned to the hillsides in surrounding areas of the town. We were instructed to walk quietly, meditatively and to stick together. One person in the group blurted out, "This is it! Our lives are about to change!" A few people laughed, and our tour leaders smiled and then began to lead us down the narrow streets to the Casa.

As we walked silently, the only sound was of shuffling feet, flip flops and a few whispers from the people in our group. A few stray dogs joined us for a while and we were asked not to encourage them to follow us all the way to the Casa.

As we made it to the gates of the Casa, the hair on the backs of my forearms and calves began to stand involuntarily at attention. There was serious energy here, and it was palpable.

When we entered the Main Hall of the Casa, there were already several hundred people there. It seemed a cross-section of the world's sick. People from all walks of life and all corners of the globe were represented. Children in wheelchairs, a few profoundly deformed people, several with newly-dressed wounds, many Brazilians, some of whom wore black or dark colors and who stood out amongst the sea of white clothing, nervously awaited instructions. Hundreds sat in the main seating area while some stood, and others crowded around a dais that was punctuated on its back wall with a large wooden triangle. Several people lined up to put photos and messages in this triangle and then placed their hands on it and rested their heads in the center while meditating or praying for a short time.

The room was buzzing with all kinds of energy and we were asked to remain quiet. A few guides took the stage to rattle off instructions over a microphone in various languages while others gave testimonials. As the room filled to brimming, it became a bit suffocating from the early-morning heat and closeness of bodies.

Suddenly João Teixeira de Faria entered the stage area from a door on the back wall next to the triangle. An assistant handed him a microphone and he looked a bit weary and slightly disheveled. He was wearing all white as well and he began speaking in Portuguese. I was later told that he gave his patented speech of "I've been doing this for fifty years. No one has been able to disprove what is happening here. I'm not the one who heals, god heals all, etc."

At the end of his speech, his body went rigid and he dropped the microphone. He seemed to have experienced an electrical jolt and then began blinking and looking around as if entering the room for the first time. His countenance changed, and the women in my group who were closest to him noticed his eye color had changed from brown to blue. I noticed that his entire body and head seemed to swell up, and he became almost imposing to behold.

Within an instant an attendant was by his side handing him a scalpel while others held trays with bandages, alcohol and other surgical supplies. A few patients were lined up on the back wall by the triangle and he went to a woman who was standing as if in a trance with her eyes closed. He gently lifted her shirt and made an incision in her abdomen and only a single drop of blood coursed down to stain her white clothing. She neither opened her eyes nor flinched.

I was standing less than nine feet away and began filming the event on my smartphone. Several others did the same and people crushed near the stage to witness. At one point, I began to feel light headed like I might pass out, not because of the operation but because of some kind of energetic disturbance in the room. To my surprise, one of the assistants who had been holding a metal tray with a bottle of rubbing alcohol on it, fell to the ground, spilling the alcohol which immediately filled the room with vapor.

Attendants found a wheelchair and quickly positioned him on it and wheeled him off the stage into an infirmary area nearby. A few others in the audience passed out as well and they were taken to the infirmary.

Toward the end of the surgery, John of God seemed to sense that there was a doctor in the audience and he regained the microphone to ask that any doctors come to the stage to witness what he was doing. A man emerged who I remembered being on my flight to Brasilia, and he introduced himself as a doctor who practiced in New Jersey. The assistants asked him to describe to the crowd over the microphone what he was seeing. Dumbfounded, the man told us in English that he was looking at a woman who was barely bleeding but had been cut fairly deep with a scalpel. To his knowledge, the woman was not under anesthesia and he had not witnessed the scalpel being sterilized beforehand. The woman was being stitched up like doctors have been doing for hundreds of years, and the doctor was at a loss to explain how this was all taking place.

John of God did two other surgeries after this. He had one woman sit in a wheelchair onstage, cover one of her eyes with her hand, and he scraped the cornea of her other eye with a scalpel while she sat silently, unflinching. A male patient experienced John of God driving 8-inch-long forceps deep into his nasal cavity and then removing some tissue forcibly. It was rather chaotic and sensational to watch all of this firsthand. I had seen videos of these surgeries on the internet, but to witness them in person — just a few feet away — was a much more intense experience. The energy in the room was another thing all together. It felt like electricity filled the air and that waves of energy were moving over us.

After all of the surgery patients had been taken to the infirmary, John of God retreated through the same door he had entered and then thousands began to queue up for "invisible" surgery. I was among them and I took my place in the "First Time" line.

Members of my tour group were herded together toward the front of the line and we waited while attendants led small groups of us go through a door in single file to the back of the Casa. Past this next door is where the "Current Rooms" were. Earlier in the morning, hundreds of people had either been instructed by John of God or had volunteered to sit in these rooms and meditate for 4-6 hours without interruption. The purpose of these rooms didn't sink in with me until much later, but from what I understand, they serve a dual purpose. They allow meditators to be healed by spirits present in the Casa, but they also become an engine room of sorts for the Casa itself. The high-frequency energy generated by hundreds of meditators is used to help John of God maintain a spirit within his physical body for several hours at a time.

For those "prescribed" to be there by John of God, their role was to sit quietly and experience subtle healing on a spiritual and energetic level. There are actually two Current Rooms and the first one you enter has been nicknamed the "Spiritual Washing Machine." Negative energies, attachments, etc. are removed in this room and it is not uncommon to see people weeping quietly with their eyes closed or looking as if they have passed out or fallen asleep. It was made abundantly clear that if we were asked to sit in these rooms that we were required to keep our eyes closed and remain silent at all times. Otherwise, we ran the risk of absorbing any of the bad energy or attachments that were being shed by others in the room. Many in our group only needed to hear this once.

The first Current Room empties into a longer, larger room that is known as the "Entity's Current Room," and at the end of it on the far left is a raised platform and chair where John of God sits. In comfortable chairs flanked on either side of him sit those who have been invited by the Entity or John of God to raise the energy of the room through meditation.

It was a strange place to be for the first time. Our group and several thousand others behind us stood quietly in a single-file line that was positioned a foot or two away from people meditating in these Current Rooms in church-pew type seats. I was so overwhelmed by all of this that I wasn't thinking about my own healing at all. We were led to stand in front of John of God at a fairly-brisk pace. Just before reaching him, one of our tour leaders came to me and asked me quietly to produce the hand-written note she had jotted down in our session the night before. I felt nervous and I didn't feel an overwhelming sense of love or healing as others had described on the internet.

I was hastily led to stand in front of John of God, and I was supposed to take his hand. I didn't even have a chance. He uttered some words to my tour leader and she pulled me away quickly so that someone behind me could stand in my place.

She leaned in my ear and said, "He said for you to 'sit in his current,'" and she led me to another area to the right of John of God that has a few more pews where people were already sitting and meditating. I sat down quickly, not having had any time to figure out what was happening to me.

I sat there numbly, feeling as if I had done something wrong. John of God hadn't even looked at or touched me when I'd stood in front of him. I had flown all the way to

Brazil for this? What if I never got another chance to stand in front of him? Now what?

I sat back, relaxed and began to meditate more deeply. I felt a palpable wave of heat and energy pass through the top of my head, and I began to think of my family — and I felt my heart open up. I started sobbing. The tears felt more out of joy, gratitude and release than anything else. It felt as if a burden had been lifted from my heart.

I had an overwhelming sense that we as humans were all being well taken care of. Everything was going to be all right. Love is the most powerful force in the universe and it is being pointed at us at every moment. We just need to take the time to open ourselves up to it. I gave thanks to John of God for being a facilitator in this piece of knowledge and to the magnificent events he was bringing about every day. It was mind boggling what was taking place here. Healing was happening on a biblical level, and I got a strong feeling that there were hundreds of spirits and beings on the other side of the veil who were there to take care of us.

After about an hour, the morning session ended, and everyone opened their eyes and retreated quietly from the Current Rooms out into the open air. We were all invited to a free lunch of "blessed broth," a minestrone-type soup that is blessed by John of God and the entities every day and is a prescribed part of the healing program at the Casa. Anyone can stand in line for a bowl of the soup and a portion of bread, and it is always free in an outdoor cafeteria area not far from the Main Hall.

I went back to the hotel afterwards to eat a full lunch there and to get more instructions from our tour leaders. They had kept tabs on everyone's progress and prognosis from

John of God, and individual instructions were given after our meal. I was informed that not only had I been asked to sit in current, I had also been scheduled for "operation" or invisible surgery that afternoon.

I felt a wave of both apprehension and excitement. This was the reason I had come, but I was being warned that invisible surgery could be tough to handle. Our leaders made it very clear to everyone who was having surgery that we needed to find one of our tour leaders waiting for us and then we would be shuttled back to the hotel in a taxi where we were required to have bed rest. I thought the cab ride was a little excessive. The hotel was only about 3 city blocks away from the Casa, and we were all perfectly capable of walking on our own, but no one questioned it and we all followed the directions.

At about 1 p.m., our group returned to the Main Hall of the Casa where we were greeted with a scene very similar to the morning session. Thousands were waiting to see John of God and buses were pulling into the parking lot. Our small group waited together by the main stage and John of God came out and spoke to the group again. He physically operated on three volunteers and I felt the same feeling of light headedness and my energy leaving me for a few seconds as the physical surgeries took place.

When John of God exited the stage and retreated to the Current Rooms, the lines began to form immediately. Very quickly, our group was herded to the front of the line and when they made the call for those getting "operation," our entire group and several others were led right through the Current Rooms to a room in back called the "Blessing Room." It was filled with church pew-like seats and could seat about 80 patients. We were all asked to turn off our cell phones, to sit quietly and to put our right hand over our heart, which would signify to the entities that we were asking for this operation.

I closed my eyes and after a few minutes, someone's cell phone rang. After a flurry of activity from its owner to shut it down, the room was quiet again, and I began to feel electrical/tingling sensations in six different places on my body. It felt like a very mild electric needle was being applied to areas on my abdomen, back and neck. Some people in my group actually reported that they had been shoved forward or to the side by invisible hands. At the end of the session, we heard John of God enter the room and bellow a blessing in a loud voice, and then we were all instructed to open our eyes and to quietly exit the room to the outside.

Those who had gotten surgery for the first time were asked to have a short orientation session with a Casa worker, and we were advised to treat this invisible surgery as if it had been a physical one. They stressed the need for rest, limited social activity, no reading or watching of TV or any electronic devices.

After the quick session, I spotted our tour leader and she grabbed a few others from our group and shuttled us off in taxis. When we got to the hotel, I disobeyed the instruction and stayed on the porch to talk with a handful of people from our group who had not had surgery. I was enjoying myself talking with them when our tour leader noticed me and rather sternly told me to go to my room.

I felt no different than I had prior to the surgery, but I figured it wouldn't hurt for me to lie down and try to take a nap. Within a few minutes of my head hitting the pillow, I was out. I did not wake back up for 16 hours!

When I awoke the next morning, I felt like I had been hit by a truck. I had no energy and symptoms were blazing. I looked in the mirror and my eyes were bloodshot, and my pupils were dilated. I suddenly had new respect for all of the rules around surgery, and I took them very seriously from that point onward.

For the next 24 hours, I was restricted to my room and was asked to stay there except for meals. The first meal was brought to me, but for the subsequent two, I was allowed to eat quietly by myself in the main dining area, and others in my group were asked not to engage in conversation with me. This all seemed to be about helping me retain my energy.

At the end of the 24-hour period, I was allowed back in the group and I began to feel a little better. I sent a few emails back home that I had just experienced my first operation, and I prepared with the rest of our group for another round of seeing John of God the next day.

CHAPTER 16:
HOLDING CURRENT

At dinner that night, our group leaders instructed us where to go and what to do for our visit to the Casa the next day. Others in our group were also recovering from their recent operations as were a few noticeable absentees who were in their rooms recovering.

I was asked to "hold current" and sit in one of the Current Rooms, which meant I would be required to sit in silent meditation for about four hours, nonstop. I had never done anything like this before, but I was up for the challenge. Luckily, I was able to purchase a seat cushion in one of the local stores after a Casa veteran highly recommended I get one; so I was prepared.

I also scheduled something called a Crystal Bed session. Several years before, the entities that come through John of God had requested a contraption be built to help balance the chakras of those being healed at the Casa. Following the precise specifications, the people at the Casa constructed these machines and have installed several on the grounds of the place. They are also for sale to the public, but only with the entities' approval. The device plugs into an electrical current and is mounted to the wall with seven arms that extend and hover over a prone patient lying on a massage-style bed below it. At the end of each arm is a 4-inch long quartz crystal that has colored light projecting through it that corresponds to the appropriate chakra.

It doesn't look like much, but I had several powerful sessions on these beds as did several in my group. Some of the older women complained that the red or green light was too hot, and our tour leaders laughed that they are all projecting at the same level of power and that if we feel any sensations from it, it means our chakras are being adjusted and an energetic imbalance is being corrected.

Our entire group retired early that night and awoke the next day at 6 a.m.

The next morning, we didn't walk as a single, united front like we had the first day. Instead, those scheduled to be sitting in current were asked to go early so that by the time the rest of the group showed up around 7 a.m., we would already be in the Current Rooms meditating.

I prepared myself mentally for what I expected be a marathon meditation session. I went with a few other group members I had befriended and we made our way into the surprisingly uncrowded main room of the Casa. The doors were opened to the Current Rooms and we quickly streamed into them and found some seats in the first room. We were instructed not to go into the Entity's Room for our first session because we were told the energy might be hard to handle.

As several hundred others filed into the meditation rooms, a Casa staff member appeared in each of the rooms to act as our instructor or motivator. They were the only ones allowed to speak and they soon asked us to close our eyes and not talk for the duration of the session. If we had to go to the bathroom, we were asked to raise our hand while keeping our eyes closed and a Casa worker would escort us out of the room in a specific way.

We were asked to recite the Lord's Prayer and Hail Mary. I was told beforehand that the Casa was nondenominational — not specifically Christian or aligned with any particular religion. I asked our group leaders afterwards why these Christian prayers were routinely recited. I was told that Brazil is a predominantly Catholic country and it was a request from the locals that these prayers be said before each session. She also said that simply saying these words raises the vibration in the Casa which ultimately helps John of God maintain a spirit in his body.

As we all settled down into silent meditation, we could hear the commotion taking place in the main room, just a few steps outside where we were seated. We could hear them singing Brazilian hymns, and it sounded like a few local residents gave their testimonies of healing. After about half an hour, the door was opened to the Current Rooms and we could hear the first group file in.

Our assigned Casa staffers gave encouraging words to us to keep us on track. They also warned us not to open our eyes and to stay focused on why we were there.

A few hours went by and I shifted in my seat every few minutes to keep my butt from falling asleep. At times, I went into deep meditation and felt like I was sinking below the surface of the water and then slowly rising back to consciousness if someone coughed or if a staff member said something out loud.

One of the women I had made friends with in our tour group was also shifting in her seat next to me and I tried to keep my eyes closed and not look at her. Another hour or so went by and then suddenly I heard the unmistakable sound of her body falling out of her seat and her skin slapping against the concrete floor. I knew I was not supposed to open my eyes, but I stole a glance to see if I was imagining this. I looked down to see her lying on her back, unconscious.

I broke all the rules at this point, opened my eyes, left my seat and tended to her. She opened her eyes to look up at me, and she seemed OK but confused. I thought my movement would've attracted the attention of the Casa staff, but it didn't. I waved my hand silently and wanted to shout out, but luckily someone noticed me, and a few staff members rushed over to my friend and admonished me for breaking ranks. I didn't know what else to do.

They quickly pulled my friend into the infirmary area which was luckily just a few steps away, and they scolded me to get back into my seat, which I did.

Everything calmed down for a minute and then I suddenly began to feel faint. I felt like whatever energy or spirit had taken my friend down was doing a number on me as well. I didn't know whether to go with it and drop to the floor or try to stay focused in my seat. I decided to do the latter, and after a minute or two the feeling subsided and I sank back into quiet meditation.

After a few more hours, the session ended in the Current Rooms, and people began to file out of the seating areas.

Several from my group were in the same area where we were meditating, and they turned around to ask me what had happened. I gave them all the info I had and when we returned to our hotel, our tour leaders told us that our friend had experienced a spontaneous "operation," which can happen at any location in the Casa. After lying in the infirmary for a few hours, she had returned to her room in the hotel where she was quietly resting and now undergoing the protocol that patients must follow after an operation.

I saw her later that night at dinner and even though we weren't supposed to speak, she gave me her account of what happened to her. She said she had been experiencing pain and was very uncomfortable sitting in the Current Room for so many hours, so she quietly prayed/requested to the entities in the room that they just get her healing over with. Within a few seconds her request was granted, and she was knocked to the ground. She said the first thing she knew, she was looking at the ceiling and wondering why that was in her field of view. When she saw my face hovering over her, she realized that she was on the ground. She wasn't in any pain afterwards and she seemed to be in good spirits the rest of our tour.

Later the afternoon of the next day, I ended up going into town with a group of friends to shop for crystals and souvenirs, and I ran into the woman I had met on my flight. She was leading a small group of her own and we didn't have time to play guitar, but I laughed that she had been right about it being easy to bump into someone in the tiny town of Abadiânia.

Also that afternoon, I had my first of several Crystal Bed sessions. Patients can pay for a single 20-minute session or a 40-minute double session, the latter being harder to book because so many people are trying to schedule appointments at the same time. I sprang for the longer sessions my first few times, figuring I had a lot of baggage to get rid of. And as it turned out, I was right. About halfway through my first session, I was overcome with a wave of fear that I was being overtaken by a dark entity and it shook me to my core. I practically ran back to the hotel and talked to one of our tour guides to ask if it was possible that a wandering dark spirit had attached to me. She said it was next to impossible for that to happen with all the positive spiritual activity around the Casa grounds, but she surmised that what I was feeling was the actual removal of a dark entity, which tends to bring up fear at the moment of removal. To be sure about things, she suggested we bring this up to John of God the next time I was in line to get his advice. As it turned out, the tour guide was 100% correct, and John of God prescribed for me a new set of "herbs" or the passiflora pills energetically encoded with what I needed to keep the dark things at bay. This was on top of what I was already taking for my previous spiritual surgery. I was asked to discontinue that prescription and start this new one. Things were getting a bit overwhelming and confusing, and I felt it was a good thing I was in the hands of people I trusted.

My second Crystal Bed session was just as amazing but in a much gentler way. Earlier in the day I had bought some quartz crystals in a local shop and found out they had not been blessed by the entities, so their healing powers might be limited. Prior to coming to Brazil, I had not been the least bit interested in crystals for healing work, but after watching the amazing power of the Crystal Beds, I was becoming a strong believer.

As I lay on the Crystal Bed and meditated, I lightly lamented I had bought these crystals instead of some others that had been blessed, and just as I thought this, I saw a very vivid image of a young nun dressed in a light blue habit. I knew this wasn't something imagined because I had only seen nuns dressed in black prior to this, and I actually thought her habit was a strange color. She was in her twenties and had very pronounced dark eyebrows that grew together into one.

She smiled at me and didn't speak with her mouth. She pulled one of the crystals from the pocket of my cargo pants and held it up to me. She gave me the understanding that she was blessing the crystal, so I didn't need to be disappointed anymore. She also let me know this particular crystal could be used for healing and as soon as she sent me that knowledge a flash of light went through the crystal and disappeared like a shooting star.

She put it back in my pocket and extracted the other crystal from the pocket on the other side. She held this one up slowly and very deliberately, and in my mind I projected to her… "I know… for healing, right?"

And she said or projected non-verbally, "No, for second sight!" A light flashed, and she put the crystal back in my other pocket. I apologized to her for being a know it all, and I thanked her profusely.

She disappeared, and the session ended about 10 minutes later. I arose to the prompting of a Casa worker who knocked on the door to let me know my session had ended, and I walked into the beautiful sunlit grounds of the Casa. Tropical birds were flying overhead, the sun was beaming through the clouds, and a light breezed sifted through my white clothes. It was a gorgeous day, and I felt that my sense of smell had suddenly been heightened because I could smell cooking food from a local posada a few blocks away. It was then that I realized every symptom of Lyme disease had disappeared. I fell to my knees and thanked god and burst into tears!

I practically levitated back to the hotel and I couldn't wait to relate my story to a group of friends who were finishing lunch in the main dining area. As I described the nun, someone blurted out, "That's St. Rita!"

I had never heard of St. Rita of Cascia, but within a few minutes, someone produced a picture of her, wearing a blue nun's habit. It was later explained to me that she was an Italian nun who lived in the late 1300s, but she later appeared to John of God in the mid-1950s when he was 14 years old to tell him he would lead a life of profound healing. Not long after his interaction with St. Rita, John of God began to heal people as he does today.

CHAPTER 17:
SACRED WATERFALL

The next morning, I was dismayed to find that the symptoms that had left me the day before had returned but to a lesser degree. I was still hopeful, however, because I could feel things were changing with me on all levels.

Since John of God doesn't practice over the weekend, our group leaders invited us to visit the Sacred Waterfall, which is about a mile down the road from the main Casa. They explained that the waterfall area is to be treated as a sacred place and there are a number of rules about it: No photography, no speaking, no removal or disturbing any of the foliage, etc. The men and women would be split into separate groups and would walk under the waterfall one at a time. This event sounded a bit like a physical metaphor for what we were experiencing at the Casa where we would "leave our burdens by the riverside" and "wash away our troubles." While I was intrigued, I treated the invitation lightly and actually considered not going and resting up in my room instead. I'm glad I thought otherwise.

A large percentage of our group met outside our hotel and we were shuttled via taxi cabs down to a staging area at the edge of the Casa grounds. We met in an outdoor pavilion area and our group leaders lead us in prayer and "setting our healing intention," and they explained more details about what was to transpire.

We walked down a rather steep pathway to reach the waiting area for the waterfall. It was paved with concrete and a few people outside our group were already using the waterfall when we got there. We heard them whoop and exclaim in another language each time they went under the water, which gave us the impression the water was pretty cold.

The tour leaders explained that the area had been blessed by the entities and that the stream ran through an underground crystal cave, so the water had an extremely high vibration.

The men waited in the concrete sitting area and the women carefully made their way down a somewhat precarious pathway to the waterfall, single file. We looked down on them from maybe 50 feet above and silently laughed as they too couldn't contain themselves when they were hit by the water. The waterfall itself is very small and maybe less than 20 feet high and the torrent of water that hits you is only about two feet across.

When the women finished, they came back up the path with their towels and every person had the same expression… big smiles and thumbs up as they silently passed us and went further up the hill.

I followed the men down the hill and we exchanged hand signals on who would go first, and who needed assistance. I was one of the last to go and I stood on the banks of the stream and watched each person go through and become invigorated by the crashing water.

Suddenly, as my eyes wandered to the sitting area where we had been, I experienced an overwhelming energetic shift. It felt like every cell in my body had been infused with extremely positive energy. I felt every symptom dissipate and this time I knew they would not return. I couldn't believe the energy coursing through me and I hadn't even set foot in the water yet! Goosebumps erupted all over my skin and I felt like I would explode like a super nova.

I turned and noticed it was almost my turn to go under the falls, so I stepped back in line. Within a few minutes, I was holding onto a crudely-fashioned handrail and stepping on some rocks in the stream that had been draped with beach towels to keep people from slipping.

I plunged my head under the waterfall and let the water hit me square between my shoulder blades as I held my head down and away from the water. I was shocked that I felt like I couldn't breathe even though my head wasn't near the water. I gasped for air and felt my entire body go into one big muscle spasm. I had no idea what happening to my body. I was experiencing paroxysms every second and then I instinctively got the idea that I was holding onto my issues. This waterfall was literally going to wash my problems away if I let it, so I relaxed and let the water hit me full force.

My muscle spasms subsided, and I caught my breath. I leaned back and let the water hit me full in the chest and then the top of my head. I could feel the trapped energy I had been harboring rush away with the flowing water. I have never experienced anything like it.

When I stepped back from the waterfall and made my way back to the people in line, I noticed that I could see my breath even though the air temperature was probably 80 degrees Fahrenheit. This place was as magical and as sacred as advertised, and I gave gratitude that I had been able to experience its beauty.

We all regrouped at the top of the hill near the pavilion and everyone started talking excitedly at once. No one seemed unfazed by the experience, and we all had expressions of happiness and invigoration written on our faces.

We rode back to the hotel via a bumpy cab ride, and it was suggested that we not take a shower right away but instead let the sacred water soak into us.

I went back to my room to go to the bathroom and as I washed my hands, I caught a glimpse of myself in the mirror. I couldn't believe what I saw, so I stepped back in front of the mirror for a better look. My reflection made me laugh out loud.

The image I was seeing was not the one I had last seen a few hours before. I looked at least 10 years younger and healthier, and it was so noticeable that I almost didn't recognize myself when I looked at all my facial features.

I laid down on my bed and pulled out my phone to have a video chat with Tracey. As soon as she got on the line she saw me and said, "What happened to you? You look different!"

I began to break down and cry with gratitude as I choked out the words, "I'm healed!" Physical healing was taking place before my eyes on a miraculous level. Her noticing my physical changes only made it more real. I *was* healed.

CHAPTER 18:
MORE HEALING

A week to the day after I had my first spiritual surgery, I was instructed to place a small glass of blessed water by my bed, give gratitude or say a prayer thanking the entities who brought about my healing and to ask them to remove the invisible sutures from my operation during my sleep. This seemed like a rather unnecessary step at first but after what I had already experienced, I had learned to take everything more seriously at the Casa. So, I followed instructions to the letter. I also remembered seeing a video of a guy in Europe who had had spiritual surgery and when doctors performed an operation on him months later, they asked him who else had operated on him because they saw signs of suture scars. The doctors were baffled when he mentioned John of God.

After returning to the Casa the second week of my visit I was once again instructed to have an operation, so this time I was prepared for what was to take place. On the day of the surgery, I went with a few other members of my group into the same Blessing Room where I had experienced my first surgery. We were all anxious with anticipation, coupled with the realization we would probably be knocked down again for a good 24 hours.

We closed our eyes in silence, placed our hands over our hearts and waited for John of God to come in and give his blessing. I don't believe any of us experienced the same intense physical sensations we had the week before, but just as John of God left the room after saying his piece, one of the Casa workers instructed us to sit for a moment and think about our family and friends back home and how we were healing so that we could return as better parents, spouses, family members, friends, etc. Something about these words cut me to the quick and I felt an energetic shift... an opening of my heart, a rush of heat and energy moving into my body, and tears streamed down my face. It was immediate and profound, and I sat motionless until we were dismissed.

As we returned to our hotel, a few people in our group were slightly alarmed that they had not felt the powerful physical sensations that they had in their previous surgery, and they asked one of our tour leaders about it. Our tour leader responded that we were all getting what we needed whether we felt it or not and that the entities tend to go out of their way to make things challenging for us at the Casa. When we expect things to go by our own plans, the entities give us what we need but in a way that turns those ideas upside down. The best thing to do is to stay in the present moment and not to compare your healing manifestations with your previous ones or with those of others. Your friend may experience a miracle healing and you may not at that time and that's not because you're a bad person or you're doing anything wrong. It's all in divine timing. The only thing that can block the healing results is your own obstructive thoughts. It's best to keep expectations to a minimum and to just stay in the experience and have faith that everything is unfolding as it should.

After lying down in my room, I was overcome by the same powerful wave of healing energy that knocked me unconscious for another 14 hours. I awoke the next day feeling less fatigued than I had the first time, but I was still rocked to my energetic core. My emotions also felt close to the surface and I sensed that my heart had been opened. I felt more contemplative about things in my life and more forgiving about events that had bothered me in the past.

After dinner the following day, I was able to join our group and our tour leaders asked if we'd like to watch a video by Esther and Jerry Hicks about the Law of Attraction. I wasn't that interested but when I heard that Esther channels a collective consciousness known as Abraham and that this group intelligence was actually behind the original idea of the movie "The Secret," my antennae went up. A friend of mine had told me a few years before to clear out 20 minutes of my day and watch the video link he had emailed me. I waited for several days and when he urged me again to watch it, I begrudgingly complied. It ended up having a big impact on me from the point of view that our thoughts dictate the type of experiences, people and things we attract in our lives. I had absorbed and adopted that idea years before with Wayne Dyer's "The Power of Intention" book and this seemed to be like that idea amplified. The only thing that bothered me about "The Secret" was its emphasis on money and financial abundance and how that seemed to be the goal of altering your thoughts and vibrations. My friend noticed that too and said that if you ignore that part of the movie, the rest was easier to digest.

The Abraham-Hicks DVD focused on the spiritual, emotional and vibrational aspect of the equation. It pointed out that we are constantly broadcasting a vibration with our emotions whether we're aware of it or not and that being aware of it can put us in the driver's seat of life — instead of simply floating adrift in the ocean of life's experiences. The Universe listens to your "rockets of desire" and always answers with a result that matches your physical/emotional vibration.

I also learned that Esther Hicks had been a major consultant of "The Secret" movie but had actually dropped out of the project when she saw the direction it was taking. Everything that was said in the DVD had an enormous impact on me and it seemed like perfect timing with all of the profound healing I was experiencing. This seemed like the perfect adjunct to keeping the wolves from my door and to maintain better health. It also gave me a new lens to examine my life and my experiences.

On the final day of my visit to Abadiânia, I was awash in a range of emotions. Part of me didn't want to leave this fantastic place and the amazing energy, while another part of me couldn't wait to get back home and share my experiences with those close to me. I had experienced nothing short of a miracle, and I had witnessed several other people in my group experience them as well.

At lunch prior to our leaving, our tour leaders felt compelled to talk to us about our "Re-entry Program."

"You have been in a place that's not like the rest of the world, and you're going back to the land of heavy energies and emotions. It's like you've been in orbit above the Earth and now you're making your way back into the dense atmosphere. You're going back to your life and situations and relationships, many of which might've brought about some of your illnesses. We want to prepare you ahead of time to meet that energy and to tell you a few things.

"First of all, it is not your job to convince people about John of God and the healing work he does here. You will waste a lot of your healing energy if you engage in arguments with your friends or relatives about that. John of God will continue doing what he's doing here regardless of how many people believe, and he doesn't need your help. He's getting plenty of it already.

"Second of all, pay attention to the life you're going back to. Look at the things that bring stress to you and try to release the toxic things and relationships that feel unhealthy to you. This won't be easy, but it will be necessary for you to maintain your health and wellness."

After that we were invited to go through a final "Bye Bye" line to have John of God bless any objects we had and of course to thank him and say farewell. According to the tour leaders, the entities who incorporate in John of God have been baffled as to why we (mainly the foreign visitors) requested such a line. To them, there is no farewell. They have access to our energies at any time and place so to them there is no reason to say goodbye. Still, because of multiple requests over the years, they obliged, and the line is offered to every tour group.

I understood the unnecessary nature of the line, but I also had some crystals and a few things that I wanted blessed, so I decided to join the rest of the group instead of sitting in Current.

Everyone who did not decide to "hold Current" went to the Casa in the afternoon and the mood seemed lighter than our previous visits. I had witnessed several people in our group have miraculous or surprising recoveries from some of their illnesses and some in our group remained silent about why they were there, so it was difficult to know what they had experienced.

It was another hot and humid afternoon and it took almost an hour to walk through the line. As I waited patiently in the queue that wove through the Entity's Current Room, I noticed my guitarist friend from my flight, sitting quietly in meditation with her eyes closed. We never did get a chance to play guitar together and I lamented that mildly as I stood a few feet away while she intently meditated and held Current. I smiled and silently wished her well, and not long after I did that she started to breath heavily, eventually heaving in short gasps.

A few Casa workers seemed to know what was happening to her and they immediately went to her side. She started sobbing and then suddenly let out several shrieks of terror, all while her eyes were closed. The Casa workers helped her out of her seat and into the infirmary area as she continued to scream with intense fear.

It was very upsetting to watch and to be only a few feet away from her while this happened. I also wondered if I had unwittingly done something to cause it. Later when we returned to our hotel, I asked one of our tour guides what happened, and she said the woman had had an "obsessed" spirit spontaneously removed from her while meditating in Current. Others might call this a spiritual possession that resulted in a spontaneous exorcism. Having seen "The Exorcist" movie when I was in my early teens and knowing that this poor woman had been "possessed" the entire time she had been leading a tour group was mind boggling.

In the next few years I would come to know this shriek and the reason I was hearing it. Several months later, while seeing John of God at the Omega Center in Rhinebeck, NY I heard this same scream when I was in the main tent, waiting to go through the line. The scream came from a woman who was sitting in one of the smaller, make-shift Current areas and I was told by Casa workers this woman had also experienced the spontaneous removal of an obsessed spirit. And a few years after this, I would hear a growl and then the scream from a friend of mine who I brought through the line at Omega. It was all very unsettling and unmistakable.

But the most extreme witnessing of this phenomenon came three years later when I was in the Blessing Room in Abadiânia, awaiting a spiritual operation. Over the course of time, I became more and more familiar with how the Casa worked, and I noticed that while many of the Casa workers came and went, some of them (who seemed more high-level) were there almost every day. One tour leader mentioned that these people were spiritual mediums and they helped with any "spiritual maintenance" that might be needed during some of the more chaotic moments in the Casa.

I saw them in action during a moment of spiritual surgery while I was meditating and waiting for John of God to come into the Blessing Room. On this particular day, the seating area in the room was completely full and four gurneys were positioned against the wall with a few patients who could not stand or sit because of their ailments.

After sitting with my eyes closed for a few moments, I became aware of the movements of a woman who was lying on a gurney. They started subtly at first but when a

Casa worker came to her side to quiet her, I could hear her put up a fight. Within seconds she began screaming with the type of scream I now recognized, and three more Casa workers came to subdue her.

In a few seconds, it turned into something resembling a barroom brawl. What was hard to understand was the woman was on the gurney because she couldn't sit or stand, but now she was kicking, punching and fighting off three grown men. I opened my eyes for a second to see what was happening and when I closed them again, I could see the spirit that had been attached to her, suddenly emerging, and it had a very nonhuman face with a beak.

I slammed my eyes shut, knowing I had disobeyed the rules of the Casa by opening my eyes, and during my efforts to follow the rules better, the fight moved off of the gurney and straight into my lap. There I sat, trying to be a good Casa citizen with my eyes closed while three men and a possessed woman slammed into me, on my lap and then tumbled out a side door into the yard.

I couldn't keep my eyes shut any longer, and as I watched the action spill out of the room and into the yard, I caught a glimpse of a Casa worker in a seat behind me with his eyes closed, making wild hand gestures in the air and apparently helping with the struggle on the etheric side.

One year later after witnessing my guitar-playing friend go through this, I actually ran into her in the Atlanta airport as we both prepared to board another flight to Brasilia. She looked completely happy, healthy and had another small tour group with her. It appeared she had entirely recovered from that crazy experience.

CHAPTER 19:
THE LAND OF HEAVY ENERGY

Later in the day, after returning from the obsessed-spirit incident in the Casa, I took an "after" picture to match the unintended "before" picture I had shot by the flowering shrub located in front of our hotel. There were no signs of swelling and I looked younger and full of energy in the new photo. In the original shot, my face actually looked asymmetrical from all the inflammation.

We took the hour-plus shuttle back to the airport and I didn't see any sign of my guitar-playing friend there or later when we boarded our flight. I got the impression that after a major event like she had experienced, she would probably stay back for at least a few days to recover.

The flight back to the U.S. was much easier on me than the flight to Brazil, but it was a shock to go from 80-degree weather in Abadiânia to snow and freezing-cold temperatures at JFK Airport. It was odd to come home to an empty house because Tracey was at work and Carly was at school. After getting settled, I went straight upstairs and took a nap.

When everyone returned home, the reunion was a little strange at first. Tracey confided that she didn't know if I would come back, based upon everything I had been through. The impact of being away from Carly for two weeks had taken its toll also. Tracey told me she had missed me terribly and that it had hurt her feelings that I felt it was OK to leave for so long. I explained that I had felt nothing but guilt for leaving her in a single-parent situation for so long but the tour leaders at the Casa tried to make us understand that those kinds of thoughts would inhibit our healing. So I let go of them, and now here I had returned better than ever, ready to be a better parent, husband, etc.

I took an extra day off of work to get my bearings and when I returned, almost everyone I worked with could notice a change in me, but they couldn't put their finger on it. "Where did you go?" everyone asked. When I mentioned Brazil, they thought I had been to Rio or to Carnival. Coincidentally, Carnival had been going on when I was there, but my experiences were the polar opposite of what that event is all about.

One of my friends who seemed to be more in tune, pulled me aside and asked, "Where did you go? You're absolutely GLOWING!" I confided in her the unedited version of my story, but to others who kept prying, I simply told them I had gone on a healing retreat in the back country of Brazil. Many knew I had been struggling with Lyme disease, so that explanation was easy to understand.

I noticed that things were getting easier at my job in general. Some people who had been antagonistic with me suddenly became easier to get along with. I knew my new vibration had something to do with this. I was much more relaxed and forgiving now, so that changed what was happening around me.

However, almost exactly three months from when I returned from Brazil, I was in a meeting in my office and I experienced an all-too-familiar brain lapse caused from Lyme. Looking back now, it is easier to understand what was happening. I had run out of the herbs I had been prescribed in Brazil and did not refill my prescription. I was also still on a single oral antibiotic, and I was beginning to slide back into some old work/stress habits. A few weeks earlier, I had gotten into a philosophical argument with both of my brothers about John of God's authenticity. I had effectively ignored two of the major rules of the "Re-entry Program" my Casa tour leaders had warned us about.

The unwelcomed feeling of Lyme symptoms returning jarred me considerably, and my immediate thought was to rush back to Brazil. Luckily, I found out that John of God was actually making a visit to the U.S. at the Omega Center in Rhinebeck, NY in the fall, so I booked reservations for both Tracey and me.

In the meantime, I simply gritted my teeth and tried to soldier through my days as each one became more symptom-filled. Over the course of the next few months, I found out about an energy healer in my area who was running a Crystal Bed. It was a Crystal Bed owned by one of my tour leaders in Brazil. She had been living in a town near me before she moved to Abadiânia permanently and she had left this bed behind. I began making monthly appointments to have Crystal Bed sessions with my new energy worker friend and after one of my sessions she mentioned matter-of-factly that Wayne Dyer had recently been healed by John of God. This news came as a pleasant surprise and seemed like an amazing coincidence to me.

I went straight home and searched online for any signs of this information, and within minutes I was watching a video of Dyer explaining that he had been diagnosed and was being treated for Leukemia when a friend of his suggested going to Brazil to see John of God.

As it turned out, Dyer was under an intense book deadline and wasn't able to make the trip, but his friend did. She was very intent upon getting him healed so she asked the entities if she could do a "stand-in" or "surrogate" surgery. This is something John of God and the entities do in rare cases when sick people are not able to travel, so Dyer's friend experienced a spiritual surgery in the Blessing Room in Brazil while he slept in his bed at home.

The next day his friend called him when he was on his way out the door to take his daily walk on the beach where he lived in Maui. She warned him he needed to spend the next 24 hours in bed, but he ignored her and started his walk anyway. He promptly collapsed about a hundred yards outside his door. It took him several minutes to crawl back to his bed and he felt that all of his energy had been drained from him. He also had restricted pupils, blood-shot eyes and felt compelled to sleep as much as possible. He spent almost a week in bed recovering from this very powerful surgery. He also mentioned that he had felt infused with love and that his ego had been removed from him.

To my amazement, all of this had happened almost exactly a month after I had had my experiences in Brazil. Within weeks I was also seeing Wayne Dyer being interviewed by Oprah Winfrey on her new cable channel, and he was very openly talking about the mystical experiences he was having as a result of his spiritual surgery. During one of the segments, he mentioned the title of one of his new book chapters — "Living Like Water" — and Oprah repeated it several times and let him know she loved the sound of it. He told her the entire book had been inspired by the ancient Taoist poem, "The Tao Te Ching," and something triggered in me instantly, and I began writing a song called "Living Like Water."

I was already writing two other songs that had seemingly been downloaded into me since my visit to Brazil — "Obrigado" (which means "thank you" in Portuguese) and "Song of Joy." I was getting this strange and overwhelming feeling that I needed to get these songs to Dr. Dyer and to have him hear them. I didn't know why but it was a strong compulsion.

A few months later, Tracey and I drove to upstate New York to attend our scheduled visit to see John of God in Rhinebeck. The people at the Omega Center did a great job recreating the environment similar to that of the Casa in Brazil. They erected a giant tent that acted as the Main Hall of the Casa and it was connected to one of their main performance halls which was divided into separate Current Rooms with partitions. John of God appeared for three days and he drew at least 1,200 people each day.

Housing and lodging was of a premium, but luckily friends of ours had a vacation house in a nearby town that was only a 10-minute drive from the center. We spent the night there prior to our first day's visit, making it easier for us to show up on time at 8 a.m. for the first session.

On the first day, we sat in the main tent and listened to testimonials and speeches from some of the Casa leaders I recognized from Brazil. At one point, John of God came out to say hello to the crowd and as he appeared, I burst into tears. It was the first time I had seen him since my visit, but my reaction surprised both Tracey and me. I felt a palpable connection to the man who had enabled a miracle healing in me.

Several hours later, we went through the line and Tracey and I were asked to go to separate Current Rooms to sit in meditation. While I was meditating, I asked for help with the music I was writing, and I saw a brief vision of a woman wearing a green and gold sash with music notes on it. Then suddenly, I was shown a vision that looked like the scene from a movie. My view passed over a CD lying on a table. It was burgundy red in color and it had a gold emblem on it. The emblem looked to be made of a flower and some sort of arc with teeth on it. I had no idea what this meant, and I forgot about it for several hours.

Later that night, Tracey and I went out to dinner and then we went back to where we were staying. While we were sitting around, talking about what had transpired earlier in the day, I remembered the vision I had been shown in my meditation. I asked Tracey for a pen and paper to see if I could sketch the emblem I had seen to make some sense out of it.

I drew the flower first and realized it looked very much like a lotus. The lotus represents "zen," I thought. Around the stem of this flower was an upward-facing arc with teeth on the outside. What could that mean?

As I started drawing the details of the teeth, I realized it looked like part of a gear. Gears are parts of engines… and then I dropped the pen. I had recently named my music project The Zen Engines. This emblem was a visual pun. It literally represented "zen" and an engine. There is no way I had come up with this on my own. In fact, it had required effort to discover what this vision meant. How incredible!

The next day, we got up early and went through the same routine as the prior day. We arrived at the Omega Center by 8 a.m. and took our seats in the large tent and waited to take our places in line. We began hearing more testimonials and then suddenly Wayne Dyer came out onstage and made a surprise visit. He began telling the same story I had seen him give in his online video, and Tracey and I just looked at each other in amazement. She also opened her purse to reveal the CD I had burnt prior to us coming to New York. It had the new songs I was working on and had hoped to give to him. At the time, I didn't know how that would be possible, but it appeared to be slowly unfolding now.

I told Tracey I wouldn't force myself on him like a crazed fan and that I would only approach him if the situation seemed right. As Dyer finished his story, he related to the audience that he had just gone through the line and John of God had said to him, "You are well." Hearing that news choked me up. It wasn't often that I had heard that happen to anyone going through the line.

As Dyer left the stage, I grabbed the CD from Tracey, put it in my pocket and then went to where the bathrooms were outside the tent. It was in the general direction of the stage, and I figured if I happened to see Dyer on the way back then it was meant to be. As it turned out, when I finished and returned to the tent door, Dyer was standing right in the doorway talking to a woman. It would be almost impossible to miss him.

I strode over after his conversation broke off with the woman, and I asked if I could have a word with him. "Of course," he said.

I told him I had seen his video online and that I had been healed by John of God almost exactly one month prior to him, but I had made the long trip to Brazil. Then I pulled the CD out of my pocket and told him, "I don't know why, but while watching your video, I had the overwhelming urge to give these songs to you."

He took the CD, looked at the titles of the songs and my name on the label and said, "Thank you, Gregg. I don't know why you needed to give this to me either, but I never question these things anymore." And he smiled back at me.

I thanked him, and he hugged me. As I walked back to my seat, I was practically trembling from some sort of energy exchange between the two of us. It wasn't from being star struck — I had met many celebrities before. This was something different. He was holding so much love and light that I had experienced some sort of transfer and it took several minutes in my seat for me to integrate it.

Later in the day, when we broke for lunch, Tracey and I were on our way back to our seats in the main tent when we ran into a woman who had been in my group tour in Brazil. She had been rather shy and quiet in Brazil, but now she seemed more outgoing and full of energy. She lived on the other side of the country so coming here must have been a bit of a chore. She had not mentioned anything about any ailments or why she had visited Brazil in the first place, but on this day, she told me she had come back to thank John of God.

When I asked why she felt compelled to do that, she revealed her entire story. She had been fighting an advanced case of Stage 4 cancer and it had spread throughout her body and into all of her bones. Her doctors had told her to get her effects in order and to prepare for her death. She probably wouldn't live longer than six months. That was her situation when she came to Brazil.

While there, I never heard her complain of any symptoms and she never told anyone her reason for going to see John of God in the first place. Now she was telling me that one night in her hotel room in Brazil, she heard a disembodied voice say to her, "You have come to reclaim the faith that never left you."

She said that not long after hearing that very distinct voice, all signs of cancer completely disappeared. When she returned home, her doctors confirmed she was cancer free, and they were baffled at her healing. I congratulated her on this amazing news, and Tracey and I both hugged her.

Later that day, Tracey and I walked through the line again and we each received a blessing in one of the Current Rooms. I was feeling pretty good, symptom-wise and was amazed how easily this whole process was unfolding.

The next day was our last day at Omega and we began making plans to head back home. We expected to breeze through the line again and to head home by lunch time.

We sat for several hours in the main tent. When we finally walked through the line, suddenly John of God announced that everyone in the line was to receive an "intervention." This is what he called spiritual surgery here in the U.S. He couldn't mention words like "operation," "surgery," etc. while here. He also couldn't perform physical operations on volunteers or even prescribe the herbs offered in Brazil. Instead, he prescribed blessed water to anyone who was directed to receive an "intervention."

Tracey and I were shocked, but I was ready to roll with this news. Tracey wasn't prepared or comfortable with receiving an intervention and it began to upset her while we were in line.

We received a quick blessing and intervention in a specific blessing area and we were escorted outside to a tent where Casa workers gave an orientation to new comers. Tracey was visibly upset, and I was already beginning to reel from the blast of intervention energy that had just hit me.

In Brazil, we would've received a free cab ride back to our hotel, but here I needed to drive us home in a ride that would take about an hour and a half. This complicated things, adding to my confusion and to Tracey's agitation.

We drove home with no incident and we were able to take a nap when we got there, but both of us needed to go to work the next day. None of this was what I had expected, but after I had a chance to take a look at the situation I realized that every time you set your own expectations on your healing, the entities do something to turn them upside down.

CHAPTER 20:
RETURN TO BRAZIL

The energy I received in New York didn't feel to be on par with what I had experienced in Brazil. So, within a few weeks of our Omega visit, I made reservations for a return trip to Abadiânia in March of the coming year.

The New York visit did curb my symptoms for a few weeks, but I felt there was no substitute for the amazing energy in Brazil. Tracey and Carly were not happy about the news that I would be leaving for another two weeks, but they were supportive nonetheless. I didn't know what else to do, and I felt like attending to my healing was the most important thing I could focus on. Of all the years of trying different protocols, this was the only thing that had had any kind of major positive effect.

I returned that March, knowing the ropes and what to expect while trying to stay in the present moment and keeping my expectations in check. And I kept returning every February or March for a few years, while also going to the Omega Center in the fall whenever John of God made an appearance.

I still felt the amazing energy in Brazil and had big, emotional moments in the Current Rooms, but I didn't experience the visible physical effects of what had transpired at the waterfall during my first visit. Symptoms were removed in more-subtle ways this time, and I began feeling some emotional/ego work taking place. My feelings were always very close to the surface at the Casa and things that would not have bothered me at home, tended to cause some surprising emotional upheavals.

I also began to see other return visitors and I made friends with them. Each time I returned I also noticed those who had stayed to live in Abadiânia. During my third return visit, an acquaintance who had seen me years before asked me in a friendly way, "So are you planning to come down here and get recharged every year?"

This wasn't meant to be a judgmental or negative question but being under the influence of that strange and powerful energy at the Casa, it flipped a switch in me. Did I actually NEED to come to Brazil every year to get recharged? Wasn't the healing happening so that I could be free of the disease and the need to return here?

It sent my mind whirling. Later that afternoon at the Casa, a Casa worker was giving her testimonial in the main hall, and she said these words, "90% come to the Casa for healing while only 10% come for the Love." She had said this in Portuguese and I asked a friend who spoke the language what she had meant because I had seen it raise emotion in her. But I still didn't understand the nature of the comment. My friend explained, "Most people come to the Casa for selfish reasons to get themselves healed, while only 10% come to experience the spiritual, loving nature of the place." The combination of these events had a profound effect on me.

I had started the Lyme disease healing quest thinking that I needed help from outside myself to completely heal. I started with Western-trained doctors and progressed through the full range of alternative healers until I ended up in Brazil. All the while I was looking for someone else to do something to or for me to bring about my healing. I realized I needed to become my own health advocate when certain treatments almost killed me, and I began to realize that there were entire groups of established protocols and practitioners that weren't designed to help my particular situation. I also developed a mistrust of physicians or healers who had no exit strategy for my prognosis and seemed very happy to charge me endless fees when I wasn't showing any signs of improvement.

Only after going to Brazil did I realize true healing was possible, but now I felt trapped if I needed to return there every year to get any kind of relief. That's when it struck me that the energy that was available at the Casa was also available anywhere in the world. It is made much more powerful there so you can recognize and understand it, but those who experience break-through healing have removed their ego and expectations and opened themselves up so they can receive and hold that love and healing energy anywhere they are.

It was an epiphany and I suddenly felt unencumbered. I asked the entities to help me remove any obstacles to my healing instead of asking them to heal me outright. I came here to learn in this lifetime and I wanted to evolve to a point to where I could heal myself and others in a way that was complete and independent.

That was my focus when I returned for a third year. On the first day of my visit to the Casa that year, an American friend of mine and I sat in the noisy main hall, waiting to go through the line to see John of God. At one point, one of our tour leaders was giving instructions from the stage with a microphone, and she made the announcement that if anyone wanted to volunteer for an invisible surgery that they should step in the line now. My friend and I looked at each other and decided to go for it. We were both there for healing and "spiritual evolution" as they called it at the Casa, so we thought we wouldn't waste any time.

As we merged into the line with hundreds of others, our tour leader saw my friend and me from her vantage point onstage. She was repeating her invitation for a volunteer healing, when she stopped and said over the microphone, "Not you, Gregg." All eyes went to me, and I began to step out of line. But it was as if an entity or someone had whispered in her ear. She quickly changed her mind and said, "Wait a minute, it's OK."

This wasn't the first time I had noticed that our tour leaders were very much in tune with the spirits at the Casa. During a visit the prior year, a newcomer in our tour group was upset because she had misplaced her passport. She ran to one of our tour leaders who said, "They're telling me it's in the side pocket of your suitcase." Everyone who heard this wondered who or what was giving the information, but the newcomer said, "But I don't HAVE a side pocket."

"No," the tour leader repeated, "They're saying you do have a side pocket and it's there." The woman ran back to her room, and when she returned, she produced her passport. She laughed sheepishly that she DID have a side pocket, but she had forgotten about it and that's where the passport was.

My friend and I stayed in the volunteer line in the Main Hall and went all the way to the Blessing Room for our invisible healing. We sat down to meditate, and several cell phones went off and were shut down within the first five minutes. Just a few moments later, John of God poked his head in the room and said a brief blessing and we were quickly escorted out of the room.

Neither my friend nor I had ever had a surgery like this before. We had barely sat down, and then we were asked to leave. He laughed on the way out the door, "I want my money back!"

With this brief experience, neither of us expected much when we returned to where were staying. Because the hotel was full, we had rented a satellite lodging house nearby. After getting the cab ride there, we both tried to make sense of what had happened.

We reached no logical conclusion so we both followed instructions and went straight to bed. We didn't emerge for another 14 hours or so. When I awoke, I found my sheets knotted in a ball at the foot of my bed. I had slept the entire time, but I had had a very restless sleep that seemed to turn my emotions upside down and my ego inside out.

My friend emerged from his room, looking like he had been pulled through a knothole and he said, "This is worse than a bad acid trip!" We both laughed out loud that we would never underestimate what was happening at the Casa again. We also vowed we would never volunteer for a spiritual surgery.

One afternoon, a friend from a prior visit found out I was at the Casa, and she asked me via email if I could walk her husband's picture through the line and give it to John of God for a prescription of special herbs. This wasn't an unusual request and I had done it for a few people in the past, but this request seemed more urgent. The last time I had seen her husband, he and I had played guitar together in the patio area of the hotel and he seemed perfectly healthy. But when I got the email photo of him, I could see he was gravely ill. I also had the strong impression that he was about to transition out of this lifetime.

I had the photo printed and I grabbed my travel guitar and laid down on my bed, thinking about what was going on with my friend. As I strummed a few chords, an entire song came through me in about 20 minutes. I recorded it on my smartphone and sent it to my friend's wife to play for him to give him comfort. The song had clearly come from outside of me and was related to his healing. Here are the lyrics:

Give me the strength to realign
Set my friends' souls alight
And ease these days coming
Like the breeze through a gentle windmill
Please let us all realign

And lead us all through the darkness
And teach us the lessons of our sadness

And if it's not time for us all to realign
Please let us all gently rise
Please let us all gently rise...

© Copyright 2012, The Zen Engines, all rights reserved

I had a difficult time recording it because I kept breaking down in tears. Some of the lyrics surprised and almost disturbed me. "If it's not time for us all to realign, please let us all gently rise?" Wasn't that saying that if it's not time for us to heal then please help us rise out of this life to heaven or wherever? And "Teach us the lessons of our sadness?" I had a hard time reconciling this, but I didn't dare edit these words that had clearly come from some spirit at the Casa.

A few days later I was back at the hotel for lunch and the tour leader who had questioned my volunteer healing was mingling with us and telling us some fascinating stories about John of God after the healing sessions. She would routinely stay with him after all of the healing lines were dismissed, and he would speak to her and the Casa staff while still incorporated. Our tour leader said in an amused tone, "Today, as he was walking to the Blessing Room to say a blessing to those getting invisible surgery, he turned to me and said, 'I will now heal all of these people… but if it's not their time, I will send them straight to heaven!'"

She was amused by this story as were the other people who heard it, but I was shocked. This was almost exactly the theme of the song that had been downloaded into me. It also helped me understand some deeper dimensions of how things work at the Casa.

It is commonly reported that John of God has a cure rate of about 85%, and I always wondered why that 15% didn't get the healing they were looking for. I believe a certain percentage is because some of those people don't follow the protocols, they go back to the same lives they left and don't make any life changes, or they let their thoughts and limiting beliefs get in the way of the healing.

I had witnessed the latter happen with one woman in an early tour group of mine. She had come to Brazil using a cane and a walker. The first time she saw John of God, he pulled her to the stage, kicked away her cane and asked her to walk to him. She walked to him to the amazement of everyone in the audience, but I was with her several days after this seemingly-miraculous event. She was crying for her cane back and was upset that she was experiencing some pain. From my own experience, I knew there was complete healing on the other side of her pain and limiting thoughts, and many of us in the group told her so. She didn't listen to our encouragement, and on the last day of our tour, she mentioned she was planning to get some invasive surgery done to help correct her problem. I couldn't believe she had gone from such a dramatic and miraculous moment with John of God to this, but everyone heals at their own pace and within their own system of beliefs. And as they say at the Casa "don't compare your own healing to others."

So, yes, maybe a few of the 15% who don't receive full healing actually hinder their own progress, but now I was coming to realize that it might actually be someone's time to leave the Earth and that John of God and the entities are not going to mess with that time table. Instead, they will assist that soul as it leaves the body to make sure it gets to the proper destination.

CHAPTER 21:
FAREWELL TO BRAZIL

By February of 2014, I was feeling almost completely healed. Using my percentage gauge of optimal health, I was in the 90-95th percentile. The year prior, I founded the Ticked Off Music Fest (www.tickedoffmusicfest.com), a Lyme disease benefit concert series that brings awareness to the issues around the disease, including unreliable diagnostic tests, elusive curatives, lack of insurance funding and the ever-growing range of co-infections that accompany the Borrelia burgdorferi bacteria. I kicked off our inaugural concert in my old hometown of Wilmington, Delaware in June of 2013, and by early 2014 I was already planning two other festivals for later that year. I did a bit of motivational speaking, appearing at my parents' Lutheran church to talk about the miraculous healing events I had experienced. I also spoke from the stage whenever we held a music fest. None of this would have been possible prior to my visits to the Casa.

I was now going to Brazil mainly for spiritual reasons and to try to hold onto the love and light I experienced there. I was also going for songwriting enhancement. Months after returning from my first visit to Brazil in 2011, I released a CD titled "Obrigado" with about half the songs inspired from my experiences in Abadiânia. I incorporated the imagery of the lotus flower and gear that had been given to me while holding Current at the Omega Center in 2011, and I also created cover art using the imagery of the sun/Creator/Aten image I had seen during a meditation years before. I welcomed all etheric sources of inspiration in the creative process and I wasn't shy about crediting them.

I felt I was ready for this healing chapter to end, and I wanted to focus on helping others afflicted with Lyme and other chronic illnesses. I booked a room in the satellite housing with two friends I had met on previous tours, and several others I knew had already reserved their rooms at the hotel. It would be a kind of reunion with most of the tour group comprised of friends I had met previously at the Casa.

It was great seeing everyone, and I was surprised to see a few newcomers in the group who had Lyme disease. One was a female U.S. expatriate now living in Europe who was being treated by a well-known American Lyme doctor. One of his philosophies intrigued me and rang true. He had told her the Lyme bacteria is very intelligent, as are the co-infections that ride along with it. They tend to run interference for each other when antibiotics are introduced into the system, and they also know to migrate from the circulatory system at the first signs of antibiotic treatment, fleeing to the organs, bones, muscle, etc. which makes the medicine ineffective. They can even change their structure, ball themselves up, and go into a cystic phase which increases their defense against antimicrobials.

However, the most interesting thing he had said is the bacteria likes the attention you give it. It likes it when you're depressed and upset about being ill because your body releases stress hormones that help the bacteria thrive. He said the best thing you could do is ignore the bacteria and try to get on with your life in short bursts. This break gives your immune system a chance to fight the infection on its own terms. I had felt this sensation in the past when something positive or uplifting had made me forget that I was sick for a few hours. I had also heard audience members at our music festivals tell me that they had forgotten they were sick during the entire course of the show, which was about six hours. Ignoring the illness and disassociating with it seemed like it was a very practical energetic shift that most people could accomplish, and I thought back to some friends of mine who had corrected me years before when I was describing "my illness."

"It's not your illness," they had wisely said. "It would be better if you didn't identify with it."

I also thought about how my own identification with the illness had evolved over the years. At first, I wanted nothing to do with it. I wanted to eliminate it as soon as possible, and I wondered what I had done in this or another lifetime to deserve such a horrible fate.

When the disease didn't go quietly, I started calling it "my disease" or "my symptoms," and I began resisting it and I became miserable. I called myself a Lyme fighter and raged against the horrible state of affairs with insurance companies abandoning Lyme patients, the Center for Disease Control not even recognizing that Chronic Lyme even existed or that infections were occurring at epidemic proportions across the U.S. I would wake up in the morning, feel symptoms and begin hating what I was going through.

It was later that I realized the disease was simply new information being introduced into my life. The illness was a doorway or fork in the road that could either take me upwards or downwards. Instead of reacting negatively, I could accept it gracefully and realize what a gift I had been given. The disease was like a forest fire that had burned away all unnecessary elements in my life while creating space for new growth. I also realized that the more I tried to fight or resist it, the more I was met with an equal amount of energy and symptoms. Understanding this, I came to a point during a visit at the Casa that whenever I felt a symptom occur, I lovingly embraced it, thanked it for the information, and then asked for it to go with love. Each symptom passed quickly after doing this.

* * * *

The first few days of my return trip to Brazil were very enjoyable. I scheduled a detox massage a few hours after arriving in Abadiânia, so I was rested and relaxed by the time we prepared to see Medium John (as the Casa workers called him) the next day.

That night before going to bed, I asked the entities something along the lines of "let's get this over with" or "please accelerate my healing and spiritual evolution." What happened after that is a bit of a blur and falls into the category of "be careful what you wish for."

I remember waking the next day and going through the line to see John of God. He prescribed a psychic surgery for me that afternoon, so I was down for the count for the next 24 hours.

When I was finally able to join my group, I remember having an animated conversation with two of my friends when I felt some solid, tiny object hit the back of my throat. Within an hour, I was feeling the effects of some sort of fast-moving cold or flu. Two other people in our group came down with the "grippe" as the locals were calling it, and they were getting completely wiped out.

In the next 24 hours, I started feeling worse and worse, and it didn't feel like any sickness I had ever experienced. I had the full-blown cold symptoms of fever, aches and pains, sore throat and cough, but I noticed that my fever seemed to be confined from the neck down. From the neck up, I felt completely normal, temperature-wise, but below that I was burning up. I felt like any vestiges of Lyme bacteria was being burnt out of me.

I also felt miserable. On my worst day I spent 22 straight hours in bed, only leaving to stumble to the bathroom. One of my roommates at our rental house had caught the grippe a day ahead of me so I looked to him for signs of what was in store for me. Unfortunately, I think I had a worse case than him, because by the time he was back on his feet, I was still flat on my back.

I missed an entire day of going to the Casa, but I wasn't concerned that my healing was being interrupted. During the prior night while I slept, several of the entities came to me in my dreams and told me they were working on me. They intimated they were healing five aspects of me and they were on the third one, and I thanked them and asked them to keep going.

However, in the middle of the next night, I finally spoke out loud, "Enough! I can't take it anymore." I cried out,

"I'm never coming back to this fucking place!" in desperation. During my sleep that night I felt concern that I was too sick to make it on a flight to go home, but then I realized that the entities would probably take their foot off my neck just in time for me to leave.

And that's exactly what happened. The morning of our return flights, I woke up with no fever and only a few cold symptoms. I still had a bit of a cough and drainage, but my energy had returned, and I was able to get most of my suitcase packed before heading to the "Bye Bye" line. Before leaving, I picked up my travel guitar and strummed three chords. The sound of them startled me. I had never played those chords in sequence before and they sounded very cool and exotic to me. Within five minutes or so, an entire song came together, and I began singing a melody that could later be turned into lyrics. What a gift this was. A song had been instantly channeled through me, and I felt it was the result of the intense physical, energetic and spiritual work I had endured.

My roommate who had also been sick was now almost completely better, and he and I had a very intriguing conversation on the front porch of our rental house before we left. He too had gone through a terrible bout with the illness and he had the same impression as me — that it wasn't a normal cold or flu. In fact, he was getting direct audio contact with spirits who actually told him they needed to "knock him down" so they could concentrate on working on him. Giving him the cold was their way of accomplishing that. He was also told he didn't need to return to the Casa to connect with the energy and healing work taking place here. He could connect with it anywhere he was if he simply opened himself up to it.

While we were talking, a fascinating thing happened. I began telling him about my own experience with the cold and he told me, "I'm being told they're laughing that you asked for things to be accelerated and they gave you what you wanted."

"Yeah, a little more than what I bargained for," I said.

"Be careful what you ask for," he replied.

Suddenly, while I was talking to him, he put his hand up to ask me to stop speaking so he could hear some distant voice.

After doing so, he announced, "I'm being told they're recommending a book for you to read." He quickly told me the book's title but was then interrupted again when we continued our conversation. And then after a third time, he went into the house to get a pen and paper.

He handed me a torn sheet of paper that read, "*Falling Upwards*' by Richard Rohr" and he said, "I was told I needed to write it down for you with the author's name."

After our conversation, my friend stayed back while I joined the others who were heading to the Casa to walk through the "Bye Bye" line. I stood with them in the Main Hall by the stage as Medium John emerged. He began doing physical surgeries onstage and the energy in the air was more intense than usual. Several people passed out in the audience as a result, including a woman from our tour group and a young Brazilian boy who looked to be about 12 years old. They were all carried to the infirmary area and I felt swept away by the high energy and chaos in the air.

Suddenly, I started getting a message. It was nonverbal, but it was the distinct understanding that the song that had just been given to me about an hour or so before would become a message and gift to my daughter. Carly was getting less and less tolerant of the two-week interruptions of my trips to Brazil and it was affecting her psychologically. I had a very strong feeling that this visit was the clincher. I also got the message that the theme to the lyrics would be that even when I'm not with her physically, I was always "here" and I saw a hand with an outstretched finger pointing to her heart.

This was a bit too much for me, and tears streamed down my face in sobs while people passed out nearby and Casa workers rushed to their aid. How would I ever be able to keep it together emotionally to write such lyrics, much less sing them… and in front of people? I asked this urgently in my mind as I was swept up in the emotion of the moment.

Hours later I was on my flight, heading back to the U.S.

CHAPTER 22:
RETURNING HOME

Upon my return, Carly was so hurt by my absence that she couldn't greet me at the door. Tracey told me she had taken this trip the hardest, and it would be an hour or so before she could face me. Tracey also asked me if I planned to keep going every year, and to her relief, I told her I didn't think I'd be going back any time soon. I described how sick I had gotten and that I had been through so much I wasn't anxious to repeat it. I also knew in the back of my mind that I didn't need to go back in order to access the powerful love and healing energy that is so beautifully revealed there.

A few days later, I was working from home, sitting at the dining room table with my laptop. I was doing this a lot more frequently, and it felt good to distance myself from the dense energy at the office. Suddenly, our Wi-Fi network went down, which was pretty unusual. I tried to restart it, but it stayed down for a while.

I took it as a sign to go downstairs to my basement recording studio and try to finish the lyrics to the song I had been given in Brazil. As soon as I made that conscious decision, I experienced a dramatic energetic shift. I had the very palpable feeling that some sort of energy force or being had entered my body and anchored itself in my heart chakra area (the middle of my chest) for about three hours. During this time, lyrics and ideas flooded into me. When the first words came — "Little darling, don't get that look upon your face. Leaves are blowing and I'll be going away" — I broke down in tears. How on earth would I ever be able to sing those words? They were too close to my feelings for my daughter!

But I was compelled to go on and the lyrics and ideas continued. I would get a few lines of lyrics, they would make tears stream down my face, and I would thank whoever was giving me this information. It took a little more than an hour, but upon finishing the lyrics, I recorded all of the vocal parts and harmonies. After listening to the playback a few hours later, I realized my voice had been affected by this energy infusion. It sounded smoother and huskier than the clean-up tracks I would record later.

These are the entire lyrics to the resulting song titled "I Will Remain":

Little darling, don't get that look upon your face
Leaves are blowing, and I'll be going away

Little darling, you know that I'm never far away
Just think of me, and you will see

That I'll be right here, and will remain...

Little darling, I don't know what else that I can say
In my mind, I'm by your side

THE GRATITUDE CURVE

Because I'll be right here, and will remain...

Dreams and hopes go up like smoke and swirl around you
I think it's strange that you have changed me
So I don't want to ever say goodbye

And now I'll be right here, and will remain...

Little darling, don't get that look upon your face
Leaves are blowing, and I'll be going away

Little darling, you know that I'm never far away
Just think of me, and you will see

That I'll be right here, and will remain
I'll be right here, and will remain
I'll be right here, and will remain...

© Copyright 2014, The Zen Engines, all rights reserved

At the end of the three hours, the energy or entity left me, and I felt a slight let-down and energy loss.

The next day during my daily meditation, I had a startling interaction. I wasn't focusing on anything in particular, but I felt the presence of a very large energy force approaching me. I couldn't tell who or what it was at first.

Nonverbally, it asked me a question. "Do you know the point of the song you were just given?" To which I replied with my mind, "Yes, that my spirit is always 'HERE' and my daughter has access to it as long as she opens her heart and thinks of me."

"The same goes for me" was the nonverbal response I received, and then it was revealed that the entity or spirit who was communicating with me was Christ Consciousness, Jesus or Yeshua, as he was known in his mortal lifetime.

Tears of understanding and gratitude streamed down my face, and my heart opened wide.

Within a little more than a month after this amazing interaction, I had pressed and released a new CD and was actually playing the music, including "I Will Remain" in front of people. The first few times I got choked up in the middle of the performance, but eventually I was able to make it through the song without breaking down. I also noticed that other songs from the CD were causing emotional triggers in me when playing. An unexpected wave of emotion would well up and cause me to blow a vocal note, so I felt I needed to be on guard when playing those first few months after returning from Brazil.

Later that spring, I was invited to play at a Pagan event, the "Church of Eternal Light Summer Festival" in Bristol, CT. Apparently the organizers of the festival had read an article written about me in a local newspaper regarding my visits to see John of God and its effects upon the music I was writing. It was interesting for me to see that not only was this message of a direct connection to spiritual inspiration appealing to traditional Christians (because I had also been invited to speak at a Lutheran church several months before), it was also appealing to non-Christian spiritualists. I loved that. Even though it was an outdoor fest, I was asked to play inside an 1880s-era former Methodist church, and I was scheduled to perform in it after a group held a guided meditation there.

The meditation session ran late and as I waited outside to gain entry, I could hear chanting and smell burning sage pouring through the cracks of the windows and doors. When I entered, the room was foggy with sage smoke and everyone exiting had big smiles on their faces. I guess something pretty cool had just happened there because the room felt light and airy.

A festival organizer helped me plug into an antiquated PA system and as I did a short sound check, a few people streamed into the room to see what I was all about. I started by talking about my Lyme story and ultimate journey to Brazil, and by the time I had finished and was ready to start playing music, the room was mostly full of people.

During my set, I noticed some faint female-sounding vocals accompanying me, and I thought it was some sort of harmonic echo coming through the clunky PA system. What was strange was each time I hit a chorus vocal part with emphasis, I would hear high-register vocal accompaniment. And it wasn't just tones I was hearing. I could hear this accompaniment was matching my vocals and lyrics with 100% accuracy and with no delay. I was concentrating more on my performance but couldn't help but notice this strange effect. When I finished my set, I answered a few questions from the audience and then promptly forgot about what I had heard.

Hours later on the ride home, my wife Tracey remarked that she thought it was cool that Carly had been singing along with my music. From the backseat, Carly said she hadn't been singing, and I confirmed that I could see that she hadn't been singing either. Carly said she thought the singing had come from another young girl in the audience seated across the room from her. I told her that I had had a direct view of the audience and hadn't seen a single person singing along. No one knew my music, so how could they follow the lyrics like that? I told them that I thought it had come through the PA system and both of my girls said they had felt the singing coming from somewhere in the room nearby them.

We all looked at each other in disbelief, and I said that I must've had some sort of unearthly help. There weren't too many other conclusions to draw!

CHAPTER 23:
TICKED OFF

For the next three years, I continued holding Lyme disease benefit concerts around the country in places like Jacksonville, FL, Annapolis, MD, Los Angeles, CA, and Honolulu, HI.

On Saturday, January 23, 2016 I collaborated with a group of like-minded people to host our first event off of the contiguous U.S. mainland. It was held in a location that most people would think to be the last place where Lyme disease could appear — the island of Oahu, Hawaii.

Even in the Lyme community, Hawaii is thought to be a bit of a "safe zone" where no ticks exist and incidents of infection and Lyme patients is nil. I admit to being of this mind when I received a call in the fall of 2015 from two Lyme patients living on two separate islands in Hawaii, inviting us to host an event there.

The first thing I asked these women was the first thing people asked me when I announced we were doing our next event in Honolulu: "Is there Lyme disease in Hawaii?" The fact that these Lyme patients were infected on the mainland and then moved to Hawaii wasn't a stretch of the imagination, and the fact that a high percentage of the islands is populated with military personnel who are getting infected all over the world and then being relocated to Hawaii was an easy thing to understand. But what about ticks?

Melissa Cox, a musician who played our very first event in Wilmington, DE and who is a former journalist and nonprofit VP, came onboard to assist, and she and I did some deep research on the current situation with ticks on Hawaii. We scoured multiple resources and also consulted with Dr. Kerry Clark from Florida who has done immense amounts of research on ticks and their effects on animals and humans in another state where Lyme disease is not thought to exist.

We found that there is an abundance of the Brown Dog Tick on all the Hawaiian Islands, and Dr. Clark has proven that this species of tick does carry Borrelia burgdorferi, the bacteria known as Lyme disease.

We also began to see more and more stories posted by Hawaiian Lyme patients on social media, many of them lamenting that they didn't know of any doctors on the islands who specifically treated Lyme. We did eventually find a few Lyme-literate doctors in Hawaii, the foremost being Dr. Kristen Coles who practices at the Steelsmith Natural Health Center in Honolulu.

We did our homework, and we wrote and posted articles about Lyme patients currently living in Hawaii. So when I received a "gotcha" phone call from a TV station in Honolulu a week before I was scheduled to fly out for the event, I was prepared.

The reporter politely asked me why I was holding an event in Hawaii when there is no evidence of Lyme disease. I politely told her that it is underreported but there are plenty of Lyme patients and plenty of Brown Dog ticks to raise concern. She then flatly asked me if I was holding this event as a boondoggle and was, in fact, raising money and then taking it off the island. I explained to her that we had been invited by Hawaiians and the money we raised was going to a patient fund to help sick Lyme patients in crisis… many whom live on Hawaii. She went silent. I suggested to her that if she was looking for a story, she would look like a hero if she reported the struggles Hawaiian Lyme patients are faced with and the potential threat of the Brown Dog Tick. I then followed up with her several times to see if she would actually report on these topics, but she and her producer ultimately declined.

I was eventually interviewed by a few local newspapers, radio stations, and I even made a TV morning show appearance with our favorite collaborator, Les Stroud from the "Survivorman" TV series.

Les has been bitten by more ticks than anyone I know and has never contracted any disease, thank god, but his message to our audience is you don't have to be afraid to go back in the woods if you've been bitten by a tick. Practice good survival skills, be vigilant of ticks and know how to extract them properly. Continue to enjoy nature.

One of the first things the morning show host asked us before shooting and then eventually on the air was, "Is there Lyme disease in Hawaii?" and of course I had plenty of things to say about it.

When the show was over, I was notified by the TV station that the Hawaii Department of Health had called the show to ask me to correct what I was saying about Lyme disease being in Hawaii. I told the people at the station that the entire reason for me coming to Hawaii was to make just the opposite point and that I could not possibly say Lyme didn't exist there. They said I could expect a call from the DOH and I told them I was happy to take it.

The next day at our event, I told the audience a story about when I was a newspaper editor in my twenties, living at the Delaware beaches. I worked for a small weekly newspaper several miles inland, and one day one of the employees told me her boyfriend kept finding Black Widow spiders while on the job as a cable installer. Black Widows are not known to live outside warm climates, but this woman told me her boyfriend was finding them in cable boxes, even during the winter months. Apparently, these boxes had electrical current running through them that gave off a bit of heat that attracted the spiders. The question was, how were they getting to Delaware?

I ended up solving the mystery and breaking the story by finding out that cucumbers were being driven up on trucks from southern states and then delivered to a pickle plant in southern Delaware. The spiders were riding along with the cucumbers and being inadvertently relocated. After I ran the article, several people came to my office and presented me with jars containing all varieties of Black Widows, many of which I didn't know existed. None of my coworkers appreciated this, and they started calling me Spider Man.

As you can imagine, when the article was published it created a bit of a stir, and I got a call from a woman representing the local hospital. She accused me of trying to create a sensation and a panic. I invited her to come to my office to gaze upon the 12 jars of Black Widow spiders I had to show her. She cordially declined and then offered to run a seminar at the hospital on what someone should do if bitten by a spider. That day the Truth prevailed.

I remarked that the Lyme patients in the audience were living proof of the Lyme situation in Hawaii, just like the jars of spiders in my office. It wasn't a very a smooth analogy but it made the point.

When I told the audience what the DOH had said, a few yelled obscenities and booed. They were all Hawaiian Lyme patients, many of whom gave us hugs and cried in our arms afterward out of sheer frustration with the situation in their home state. One of them was a woman from Maui who claims to have been infected there.

My goal always has and always will be to get the truth out about the slippery slope of Lyme disease. It's not to freak anyone out, scare them or to be angry with those who don't take the time to understand. The more people are armed with the knowledge of tick awareness, the more they can practice Lyme prevention. The more people know how to recognize and treat early-onset Lyme, the more they can avoid chronic Lyme. And the more people know about chronic Lyme, the more they can avoid being misdiagnosed with ALS, MS, RA and a host of other diseases that Lyme illiterate doctors are diagnosing out of convenience because they don't understand the complex nature of tick-borne diseases.

CHAPTER 24:
LYME PATIENCE

Because of my experiences with the benefit concert series I was hosting, my attitude was changing about what the Lyme community needed and was asking for. There were several larger institutions raising funds for awareness and research, which had been my original charter. Seeing that they were raising millions of dollars made me feel like the amount of money I was raising was a drop in the bucket, and I was seeing and hearing something from the Lyme patients themselves that changed my way of thinking.

When I first started holding the concert events, I expected the majority of the audience members would be non-Lyme patients who would be more interested in the music, finding out about the cause, and donating dollars. Instead, I found that about 80% of the audience was routinely comprised of Lyme patients. They were showing up in wheelchairs, walkers, etc. and were being invigorated by the music the entire extent of a six-hour show.

Many of these patients were there seeking help. They simply showed up to our Lyme events to get more information on doctors and treatment because they weren't getting it from any local sources. Their doctors were bewilderingly ignorant and even hostile about believing that chronic Lyme disease was really just some sort of psychological disorder and a figment of the patient's imagination. These patients had seen the advertisement for a Lyme event — never mind that it was mostly about music — and were attending to plead for help. I was paying attention.

By the time we did our fourth event, I was already preparing a Lyme disease nonprofit patient fund to directly help these patients. There were a handful of patient funds already in existence and the larger ones were helping mainly children. I decided to step into the breech and focus on helping adults and the parents of these children.

In December of 2015, I launched Ticked Off Foundation, Inc., which is a Lyme support organization designed to provide financial assistance and support to Lyme and tick-borne disease patients over the age of 26 who are in crisis. We do this through grants and counseling in an effort to stem the tide of Lyme-related suicides. According to Dr. Joseph Jemsek (MD from Washington, DC), "The most common cause of death in Lyme disease is suicide." Through our efforts and support through donations and sponsors, we hope to put this reality in the past. The organization is now recognized by both the IRS and State of Connecticut Franchise Tax Board as a tax-exempt 501(c)3 organization, EIN: 47-4783824, and contributions to the Ticked Off Foundation are tax-deductible as allowed by law.

I was also seeing another unexpected phenomenon at the concert events. Because of my past experience running all-day concerts and music events for the magazine I ran in

Delaware, I was a stickler for musical quality. I hired the best local and national bands who were sympathetic to the cause, and I found some of the best musicians in the country who were also suffering from tick-borne diseases. They told their stories from the stage, as did I, and then played an extra-inspiring set of music that had obviously been influenced by their struggles. These events became extremely emotional experiences and many audience members were moved to tears.

After these shows, audience members would grab me and confess they had forgotten they had Lyme disease the entire course of the show. One woman in Annapolis gleefully told me she had not seen her sick daughter smile in six months. She said that's all she had seen her do the entirety of the show. It was moments like these that let me know I was on the right track and that there was more to running a Lyme disease event than raising awareness and money — at least for me.

CHAPTER 25:
DEEPER INFORMATION

After returning home from Brazil in the winter of 2014, I began pouring myself into books of a certain kind. Because of my supernatural experiences, especially with disembodied entities, I was more and more interested in books written by authors who claimed to have gotten their information from a source outside themselves — either through channeling, direct contact or "divine" inspiration.

These books included "Power vs. Force" by Dr. David R. Hawkins, "The Untethered Soul" by Michael A. Singer, "The Law of One" series by Elkins, Rueckert & McCarty, "Journeys Out of the Body," "Far Journeys," and "Ultimate Journey" by Robert Monroe, "Convoluted Universe" series by Dolores Cannon, "Anna, Grandmother of Jesus," and "Anna, Voice of the Magdalenes" by Claire Heartsong & Catherine Ann Clemett, and "The Hathor Material" and "The Magdalene Manuscript" by Tom Kenyon.

I also took the advice of the spirit who had spoken through my friend in Brazil (who I think was Mary Magdalene) and read the book "Falling Upward" by Richard Rohr.

At first, the books that had the deepest impact on me were the ones related to Christ's early life and the Essenes. I hadn't forgotten what the psychic friend had told me in Delaware that I had been an Essene in a past life. And I didn't feel it was a coincidence that I was having physical reactions while reading books on this subject. After reading "The Magdalene Manuscript" by Tom Kenyon, I remarked to my friend who runs the Crystal Bed near me in Connecticut, that I was deeply stirred by the book and she told me she had another book that should have the same, if not deeper, effect. She gave me "Anna, Grandmother of Jesus," and within a few chapters, I was experiencing physical reactions.

Learning of Christ's "missing years," (the days between his infancy and re-emergence in his late twenties that are not mentioned in the New Testament) was both fascinating and familiar to me. The philosophies and way of life of the Essenes who served as the support group and extended family where he grew up also struck a deep chord in me.

Finding out that Yeshua's mission to provide an ascended example of how all of us can be, made a lot more sense to me than the biblical depiction that he "died for our sins and we need him as our savior." He specifically taught the opposite of that and literally said the "kingdom of heaven is within you" and that each of us can do what he did and possibly take things even further.

While reading these books, I could feel waves of energy pass over me, and I would sometimes feel compelled to take a nap after a particularly mind-blowing chapter. I was told that there is actual encoding between the words and that if I read the books a second time, it would be an entirely different experience. It was, amazingly. After re-

reading them, I couldn't believe the incredible things I had missed the first time, and I had even stronger physical reactions during the second readings.

I had the same reaction to Tom Kenyon's "Hathor Material." I began reading the book about a month before attending a performance/workshop of his in Manhattan in the summer of 2015. After finishing one of the chapters, I put the book down to go upstairs to get something, and before I reached the top of the stairs I was overcome with a wave of heat and energy and I almost passed out. I made it to the top of the stairs and laid down to see what would happen. I felt as if some outside source was downloading information into me subconsciously. After taking it all in for about 20 minutes, I stood up and everything was back to normal.

A few weeks later, I attended Kenyon's event at a theater in Manhattan. The audience and I witnessed his amazing singing meditations where he summoned angels and ascended beings. After one of the meditations, a man who had been sitting quietly next to me suddenly introduced himself and looked at me sideways as if to say, "Don't think you can hide your secret from me!" During the intermission, we all adjourned and walked outside, and this man made a point to re-introduce himself. This time he said, "Thank you for your gigantic angelic presence!" I was completely unaware I had done anything at all!

Later that summer some neighborhood friends of ours introduced me to a relative who was a practicing psychic for a living. I was given his phone number and within minutes of me calling, he started scanning and reading me over the phone.

After telling me a number of things that let me know he was authentic, I half expected him to say, "OK, that will be $150!" but he didn't. In fact, he said that I could call him any time and that I was someone much like him, a part of the team as it were.

As I began thanking him he interrupted me and asked, "Do you have an antique mirror in your house?" When I told him I did, he asked where I had gotten it. I explained that the mirror was originally part of a chest of drawers and it had been in the attic of a house we had bought. The previous owner told us we could have anything in the attic when we made the purchase. I saw the large mirror, which spanned about 4 feet in width and had a large, dark wooden frame that was about 5 inches thick, and I removed it from the chest of drawers that we eventually threw away. I loved the mirror and the fact that it had an authentic antique look about it.

The psychic told me that the mirror had the trapped spirit of an angry old man in it and that this entity wandered the halls of our house at 5 a.m. or so. Aside from that being extremely creepy information, I also hated the fact that he was saying disparaging things about the mirror that I liked so much.

While he was explaining that I needed to get rid of the mirror, I began thinking that I wasn't going to get rid of it. Instead, I would sage smudge the hell out of it and do a bit of modified Reiki to release whatever spirit was inside of it. I had done this with people, so an object should be even easier.

Suddenly, the psychic stopped what he was saying and said, "I'm being told you think you can remove the spirit yourself, but you don't know how to do it the right way and you'll only make things worse."

Now this guy had my full attention. I asked him what I could do to cleanse this mirror. He recommended I seek out someone who was an expert at removing spirits and that in the meantime I needed to cover the mirror with a blanket and put it in the basement facing the wall. I followed his instructions to the letter, but that night, Tracey, Carly and I all had trouble sleeping because we all felt some sort of presence wandering around our house.

I had no idea how to go about looking for someone to exorcise my mirror, but within a week, my friend who runs the Crystal Bed recommended someone to me.

This spirit-remover came to my house one hot summer afternoon after a few phone conversations. She brought with her a suitcase of accoutrements. She asked me to put the mirror face up in the center of our backyard, and she sprinkled salt around its perimeter. She also lit some sage and created an altar of sorts there in our yard. She asked me if I was going to witness this event or if I'd like to participate. I told her I was very interested in learning to do what she was about to do, so she handed me a Native American drum and I followed her instructions.

We began beating drums and she started singing Native American chants that were punctuated with woops that I'm sure made our neighbors on three sides of us wonder what the hell we were doing. After this, she asked me what my spirit animal was, and I realized I had never discovered this. I had seen plenty of animal totems for other people but had never taken the time to do this for myself. She told me we would figure it out right away and as we stopped to meditate, we both saw a raven. She pointed out that this raven was not my true spirit animal, but it had appeared to serve our purposes for this cleansing event.

We began beating the drums again, but this time we were meditating while doing so and I saw a large swirling column appear around the center of the mirror that rose up like an inverted tornado. I saw that it was pulling things out of the mirror and up to the light while the raven circled above it.

When we were finished, I mentioned this vision to the spirit-remover and she confirmed she had seen something very similar. She also explained more about the story behind the mirror. She said there was also the spirit of the old man's daughter in the mirror and that's why he had been so angry and bitter. She had died suddenly at a young age, and apparently, the mirror was in the room when she passed, trapping some of her energy as she left her body. The same thing happened to the old man when he passed. The spirit-remover told me that both spirits had been removed with love and the mirror was now clear.

After I mentioned this strange experience to a few friends who were open to this kind of discussion, some of them confirmed that it is a custom in some cultures to put veils over mirrors or turn them to the wall when there is someone in the house about to pass to the other side. After hearing my story, my friends no longer thought that covering mirrors was a silly superstition!

CHAPTER 26:
HEALING IN AMERICA

By the spring of 2015, after kicking off the Lyme patient fund, I was hearing from about half a dozen very sick Lyme patients per week. They were people who had run out of money, hope and ideas on treatment. Many were suicidal, and it was a lot for me to be taking these calls all hours of the day. It took my full attention and loving patience to hear all of these horror stories and to only have a limited set of tools to help these people. Donations were slow in coming and I didn't have much money to help supplement many treatment plans. So, I did what I could and acted as a free counselor.

I began to hear a pattern, and a group of people emerged that I hadn't been exposed to before. Several patients had become so mold sensitive or sensitive to electromagnetic radiation that they had fled their homes and began living in their cars, hotels or even tents. They also became so sensitive to treating their illnesses that they could only take the slightest dosages before being plunged into an all-day Herxheimer reaction.

It dawned on me that these particular patients might respond well with energy healing, considering the fact that physical healing seemed to be almost entirely out of the question. So, I started offering remote Reiki sessions to these individuals.

I also began inviting patients to join me in seeing John of God at the Omega Center in Rhinebeck, NY when he made his yearly appearance there. The experience was very different from being at the Casa in Brazil, mainly because John of God and his group of assistants only visited for three days in New York. And even though the energy and experience seemed to me to be a lighter version of what I experienced in Brazil, as the years went by, the energy and intensity of healings became greater.

The first year I began bringing Lyme patients through (which was my second year of attending the Omega Center event), I brought through a Lyme friend who was wheelchair bound. She was going through a lot of emotional healing, was still on long-term antibiotics and was also experiencing frequent seizures.

I pushed her through the line in her wheelchair and when instructions were given by John of God for my friend, I didn't hear anything about me. I was feeling Lyme-free at that point and figured I didn't need an intervention — not hearing anything prescribed specifically for me seemed to confirm this.

So on the afternoon when a spiritual intervention was prescribed for my friend, I wheeled her into the makeshift blessing room and parked her in the perimeter of the room with the other patients in wheelchairs. At first, I sat in the gallery and was careful not to place my hand over my heart to give permission for an intervention. I felt I didn't need one and it had not been directly prescribed for me.

But before the intervention got started, I actually got up from the gallery and stood by my friend so there would be no confusion about me getting an intervention "by accident." I should've known there is no such thing as an accident there.

After John of God came into the room and gave his blessing, we were asked to open our eyes and begin filing out of the room. Since it was my friend's first intervention, I needed to wheel her over to the orientation tent to get her instructions on next steps in her healing. When I looked down at her, I thought she had died! She was slumped over and seemed unconscious.

I positioned her in the tent and sat down next to her and gently nudged her to see if she was OK. She awoke very quickly and as her eyes began to focus on me, they widened, and she said, "You did TOO get an intervention." She knew I had not necessarily wanted one. "Look at your eye. Oh, my god!"

I left the tent and hurriedly went to one of the nearby bathrooms and looked in the mirror. What I saw in my right eye seemed like a deliberate attempt by a spirit to let me know someone had been working on me. There was a very interesting bloodshot design in my eye that looked anything but natural. There was a pin dot with a perfect circle around it so that nothing was in the center but the pin dot. On the outside edges of the circle were rough edges that radiated out that looked like spin art I have seen at county fairs. I have never seen anything like this and there seemed little question that I had received an intervention, but I knew of one other deciding factor.

"When I take us home, you need to go to bed right away," I told my friend. "I'll also lie down for a while and if I don't wake up for 14 or so hours, I'll definitely know that I've had an intervention." And that is exactly what happened.

We both woke up the next day feeling pretty rough and knowing we had gotten a healthy dose of energetic healing on all levels.

By the third year, when I called my friend to see if she wanted to return for her third visit at Omega, she politely declined. She confided that she was feeling so healthy that she was driving again, was having no seizures and was way more functional than she had been in years. "Take someone else in my place," she suggested.

So I did, and I actually brought six Lyme patients through who were all in varying degrees of symptoms. One was in a wheelchair while the others were suffering from milder but persistent neurological symptoms that included fatigue. One patient was a young guy in his twenties who flew in from the Midwest for only one day. He was having trouble fitting it into his schedule and he was fixating on finding all-white clothes and having trouble finding them in stores. I told him that as long as the clothes were a light color, he didn't have to follow each rule to the letter, and the important thing for him was to show up and to let go of his expectations.

On the day I met him, which was the last day of the event at Omega, our group had already been through the line and had interventions during the first two days. This was unheard of. In the past, it was more common for patients to go through the first two days and receive blessings while only getting interventions on the final day. I began letting the patient group know that that's what they might expect, with the caveat that the entities like to turn things upside down for people. All rules and expectations were changed that year. Plus, the energy being brought forth was extremely intense.

The first day we went through, John of God sent people immediately to the intervention area and gave them interventions on the spot. I had never seen that before. As patients filed out of the intervention area, they grabbed blankets or took off their jackets, threw them on the ground and began to take naps right on the lawn of the Omega Center. Everyone was getting knocked out by the healing energy and there was no mistaking it. This was visible proof that patients who had been bubbly, talkative and anxious minutes before, now looked like they had been drugged. Of course, they hadn't, but their eyelids were heavy, they were groggy, and they couldn't wait to find a place to lie down.

So, as I met the young guy from the Midwest and had him sit down with our group, an announcement came over the PA that John of God was offering interventions to everyone waiting in the tent. That meant about 2,000 people. I had also never seen this before.

I wasn't completely surprised by this, based on how things were going that year, and the young guy started peppering me with questions. People in front of us began shushing us so they could hear further instructions from the stage, so I told my friend that everything would be OK and that he should just relax and go with the energy.

He was having physical Lyme symptoms that included a pain in his knee and he was hoping the healing could focus there. I told him that there were probably underlying factors involved and that he should stop trying to focus on details for the time being.

We all went through the line and after our interventions, we all felt groggy and the need to go home to bed. I asked my friend to stay in touch and to let me know how he was progressing in the next few weeks. I said the same thing to the rest of the group because we wouldn't be seeing each other after this. We'd all be sleeping for the next 12-16 hours and then we would be getting up and returning home.

About a month later, I texted my friend from the Midwest and I asked him how the Lyme symptoms were and if he needed any further physical support from some healing herbs I knew about, and he said he was "all set." When I asked him to explain, he called me.

"Yeah, I'm good," he said when we connected on the phone.

"So, your knee is better and you're not in any more pain?" I asked.

"No, it's a little better and I still have some pain. But I'm all set."

"What do you mean?" I asked.

"Well, one thing I didn't tell you is that I had a brain tumor," he confessed. "I didn't want to make a big deal out of it when I was in New York. But the week after I got back from seeing John of God, I felt some drainage coming out of my nose and it scared me. I thought I was hemorrhaging and dying, so I called the hospital to make an appointment for surgery. I was prepped for surgery and lying on the table when the doctors made one more scan to see the size of the tumor they'd be operating on. When they saw the results of the scan, they walked in the operating room with these crazy looks on their faces. They couldn't find the tumor. It's gone! So, I'm all good. I think the healing energy is going to take care of my knee, too!"

I had nothing to say but, "Wow, I agree. I think you're on the right track!"

CHAPTER 27:
BREAKING OPEN

In summer of 2015, something new and exciting presented itself. From that June for almost an entire year, I began receiving full music downloads from some outside source. This was different from anything I had experienced before. I wasn't getting a snippet of music or simple inspiration. I was actually hearing songs as a channel every three weeks or so. It was occurring so rapidly that I would still be in the middle of finishing the recording of a particular song I had just received the week before, when a totally new one would come into the picture and interrupt me.

The interesting thing about these songs was that they followed no coherent style. One week I would get a quasi-heavy metal song and then three weeks later I would get a quiet, folkish tune. On Christmas eve of 2015 I received an entire Christmas song, much to my chagrin. I have to admit that sometimes I resisted this inspirational download, but after I received the complete information, I found it irresistible. The Christmas song, for instance, caught me completely off guard because I had always thought it was pretty cheesy for a modern musician or group to write a gratuitous Christmas song to cash in on the holidays. When I got mine, I figured I would shelve it after finishing the writing and recording of it. But I found the more I resisted and the longer I worked on the tune, the more I began to enjoy it. This ended up being a good exercise for me because I began taking whatever came my way as a music channel and vowed that I would no longer try to filter anything. How ungrateful could I be? This was a magical gift and I shouldn't question or turn up my nose at what I was getting!

Then something pretty staggering happened, at least to me. On January 10, 2016, David Bowie died at the age of 69 after a bout with cancer. I wasn't exactly a fanatical fan, but I had bought a few of his albums back in the day and I thought songs like "Fame," "Golden Years," "Ashes to Ashes," and "Space Oddity" were works of genius.

The day after Bowie died, I woke up with the song "Moon Age Daydream" in my head. I hadn't heard that song in years and had even forgotten it existed. I thought it was pretty weird that it seemed to have independently placed itself in my head as the first thing I thought of when I awoke. For the next week, I received a new and equally-interesting Bowie song upon arising each day.

On the eighth day, I didn't wake up with a song in my head. But as I was making coffee that morning, I started hearing a new song that I had never heard before. It had Bowie's voice singing it, but I didn't recognize the tune. Suddenly, I realized what was happening and I ran down to the basement to get my acoustic guitar and tried to match what I was hearing in my head. The song slowly unfolded over the next three days or so, and I was surprised by everything about it — the chord structure, lyrics and instrumentation — all were unfamiliar but very cool to me.

The most satisfying thing about it is the song picks up where the Major Tom saga left off. In fact, it's about Major Tom returning to Earth to herald the spiritual ascension of the planet. Here are the lyrics:

"Astronaut"

It's such a subtle secret, I hope that you can keep it
I speak it when you're dreaming, have you embraced the meaning?

It wasn't my decision, to come here on a mission
Recovered from the wreckage, to bring you all a message...

You are not alone, I am always here, listen what I say
You are not alone, I am always here, we hear what you say

An interstellar DJ, who came in on the short wave
To interrupt this program, with tales of the Starman

When circuitry was spotty, I traveled out of body
Light years beyond the Black Sun, to show you that we're all one

You are not alone, I am always here, listen what I say
You are not alone, I am always here, we hear what you say
    And now it's time to fly away...

And now I need to mention, this cosmic intervention
It's time for me to meet you, to blow your minds and greet you

You are not alone, I am always here, listen what I say
You are not alone, I am always here, listen what I say
You are not alone, I am always here, listen what I say

THE GRATITUDE CURVE

You are not alone, I am always here, listen what I say

© Copyright 2016, The Zen Engines, all rights reserved

As this song came together, I began adding cellos, violins, gongs and other instrumentation that I didn't routinely use on my music.

The weirdness continued a few weeks after the song was finished. One morning I woke up with a particular snippet of David Bowie's "Blackstar" song in my head. It is the title track to the album Bowie released in January on his birthday two days before he passed. The album's lyrics are rife with references to his impending mortality. I was somewhat familiar with the song and had seen the video a few times, but I didn't know the lyrics very well.

The melody to the refrain kept playing in my head and it prompted me to go online and find what the lyrics were. Here they are:

> Something happened on the day he died
> Spirit rose a metre and stepped aside
> Somebody else took his place, and bravely cried:
> (I'm a blackstar, I'm a starstar, I'm a blackstar)

© Tintoretto Music

I didn't know what to think about this. Was I getting messages directly from Bowie explaining things to me about the day he died? Was he telling me I am the blackstar? Was he referring to the character in the song he gave me? What the hell?

Almost exactly a year later, I had the sudden urge to find out if all of that had really been a direct interaction with

David Bowie, and I realized how I could confirm it. Years before, I had made friends with a British woman who was living part-time in Abadiânia, Brazil not far from John of God's Casa. One afternoon after exchanging wild spiritual stories, she confided she was friends with a woman who had somehow gained the ability to hear the voice and thoughts of a very famous rock star who had passed in 2012. She introduced me to her via email, and soon after I began communicating with her directly.

In 2014 after the experience I had when an entity entered my body to help me write a song for Carly, I asked this friend what her rock star friend's perspective was from his side of the veil. And I asked him if he could help with the song in any way. Here is what he said:

"Gregg, I like your song and I'm glad you are letting your pain inspire your art. I will be happy to add a little dash of my magical Healing Love Elixir to the mix. But you don't need it. Music is one of the best medicines there is. Music is vibration and when somebody responds to a vibration and lets it lift them up, they move closer to perfect health. Someone who is ready to be healed will be healed as if by magic. Someone who is ready to believe that healing is possible will move closer to being able to accept healing."

Here it was almost three years later, and I was asking a similar question. This time I posed to him, "Was it David Bowie who helped me write that new song?"

His response was, "You know better than anyone who the source of your inspiration is. Were you thinking about Frank Sinatra when this song came to you? We dead musicians do this all the time. We love it when we find someone who is receptive and will run with an inspiration we offer. But he didn't do the work for you so it's really your song. Inspiration is free. No charge."

Then he said something that took all of us by surprise. He mentioned that a few years ago he had given my friend the words to a song. The song had been inspired by his experience of being in a coma before he passed. While comatose, he had traveled to a dark place and ended up in a new world he didn't know existed. He put this experience into words and gave it to our friend.

"Alas, she can't hear music in the air like you can. Would you like to try writing the music for it? I'll help of course. Okay. Listen to some of my songs, the old ones especially. Look at some pictures of me to focus your attention. I'll have her send you the lyrics in a while. Okay?"

We were all dumbfounded. Of course, I said yes, and I was 100% into this kind of experience. My friend confessed that this had caught her off guard as well, but she was also on board.

About a week passed and I hadn't received an email or any kind of message with the lyrics, so I remained patient. But one morning I woke up with a very specific melody in my head and just as I opened my eyes, I had the visual impression of our rock star friend's face.

I went about my day and kept remembering and then forgetting the melody line. It was so distinct I was sure it was from a song I had heard on the radio, so I kept disregarding it. Finally, I decided to figure it out on the guitar when I realized it wasn't going to leave me alone. And when I did, an entire song cascaded after it. I knew instinctively that this was my rock star friend downloading the song into me. As I was finishing it up, I got a text message from my friend in perfect synchronicity. She sent the lyrics and I told her the song had already come. It didn't happen like we thought it would, but it happened. She asked if the lyrics fit the music, and when I sang to them with the melody line I had been given, they matched about 90%.

It took a few weeks to get it all recorded and then I sent a link to a rough version of the song for my friend and rock star friend to review. I didn't hear back for more than a week and I started to feel nervous. What if they hated it? What if I didn't do the song justice? What if the song hadn't come from my rock star friend? That would make me question my accuracy and even sanity! A few weeks later I sent another version of the song that had a better mix and then I got my response when I asked if they liked it.

"YES! It's happy and a little bit spooky! I love it! I love it!" is what my rock star friend said. I heaved a sigh of relief and put the offer to both of them to do more of this kind of collaboration because I really enjoyed it.

I eventually compiled all of the songs I received via channeling into a download-only album titled "Break Open" and I released them in January of 2017 and have been playing all of these songs live in performances throughout the country.

CHAPTER 28:
THE SIX STAGES OF HEALING CHRONIC LYME

By 2017, I had spoken with thousands of Lyme patients and was starting to notice some patterns. Most patients were going through the same issues, especially in the early stages of diagnosis and initial treatment, and the ones who healed completely all experienced a remarkable number of similarities. The patterns reminded me of the "Five Stages of Grief" system originally developed by author Elizabeth Kübler-Ross.

In 1969, she published her book "On Death & Dying," and in it she presented a famous formulation of the stages of grief that dying people tend to go through as they approach their expected and impending demise. Since the book's publishing, her stages-of-grief system has become more popular than her book, and it is now a part of our modern cultural awareness. The five stages include denial, anger, bargaining, depression and acceptance.

Inspired by Kübler-Ross' work, I began to notice similar but different stages of consciousness, experiences and emotions for chronic Lyme patients as they move to complete healing. One of the differences in the staging system I developed is that a patient can get stuck in a stage and never progress to complete healing. Conversely, in the stages of grief, a patient ultimately moves through the system and reaches the final conclusion of death whether they like it or not.

Another difference I've noticed, is that the chronic Lyme patients who progress to 100% remission experience a shift in consciousness that can be tracked in a hierarchy. I would like to make a fine point that I'm talking about chronic Lyme patients exclusively. I'm not talking about early-onset Lyme patients who have gotten a timely diagnosis and have taken a round of antibiotics or herbal treatments within the first 60 days of infection that completely disabled the disease. These people can go on with their lives mostly unfazed. It's the chronic Lyme patient who must go through these six stages to make it to complete recovery. It is a much different and more challenging experience and not everyone makes it through. In fact, it is rather rare to do so.

I would also like to point out that this staging system attempts to describe the experiences of people who have recovered from chronic Lyme whom I've had direct experience with. I am open to hearing about any chronic Lyme patients who have fully recovered in different ways, and I understand that no staging system can be entirely comprehensive.

Also, chronic Lyme patients may experience these stages in a different order than presented here. That said, this system seems to adequately describe the steps a typical chronic Lyme patient goes through on their road to complete recovery.

Discovery:
Patients can get stuck in this stage for months, years and even decades. They know something is wrong with them, but they don't know exactly what. They go from doctor to doctor and take test after test and still don't reach an adequate explanation for the wide range of symptoms they're experiencing. Or worse, misdiagnosis may send them down a treatment rabbit hole with no end solution. When a definitive diagnosis does come through, the patient feels an overwhelming sense of relief that they can now focus on their disease with a treatment that will ultimately bring them to complete recovery. For the chronic Lyme patient, this relief is short-lived as they begin to experience the challenges of the Treatment phase.

Disillusionment:
This stage may come during the Discover stage or during the Treatment stage. Either way, a chronic Lyme patient will begin to have some of their beliefs about their trusted medical systems, insurance coverage and Western medical doctors' knowledge overturned. Every chronic Lyme patient expects to go to a trusted physician, get a timely and accurate diagnosis, and begin an effective treatment protocol that completely eliminates the illness. This is the process that helped them recover from colds, flus and other acute illnesses, so why wouldn't this work for Lyme disease?

As the chronic Lyme patient begins to experience inconclusive or incorrect diagnoses and treatment protocols that are dangerous and ineffective in curing them, they lose faith in the system that had supported them in the past. They find that insurance companies don't cover alternative treatments at all and barely cover pharmaceutical treatments that often don't help. Many of their doctors have not been trained in chronic Lyme treatment so these physicians can become defensive and question whether their patients are sick with a legitimate disease. Family members may begin to believe that the chronic Lyme patient's illness is all in their head and that the patient is either seeking attention or suffering from depression or mental illness.

At this point, the patient who can move from disillusionment through a belief-system shift of self-empowerment (by becoming their own health advocate or even their own physician) is the patient who can move up in the hierarchy.

Treatment:

Treatment of chronic Lyme is not a one-size-fits-all proposition. Physicians and patients are finding that the treatment combinations that work effectively tend to be customized to the patient and their set of symptoms and co-infections. It is important that a patient goes through the Disillusionment phase by realizing that the scenario they experienced in the past of diagnosis/treatment/cure will not be the same straight line with chronic Lyme.

Further confusing is the fact that because antibiotics are prescribed and proven effective in treating early-onset Lyme, many physicians prescribe antibiotics-only treatments to their chronic Lyme patients. These patients may experience some early symptom relief, but many cannot tolerate antibiotics alone or find that they need to continue treatment when their symptoms return weeks, months or years later. Most physicians agree that while antibiotics-only treatment may give some relief, it is not a cure for chronic Lyme disease.

The patients who reach complete healing move to all-natural and herbal remedies to remove the pathogens with a combination of detoxifiers that allow them to eliminate toxins from their system without suffering from endless Herxheimer reactions. At this point, it can be an important move for a patient to do their own research and find the treatment combinations that work for them. This move to self-empowerment can help guide them through the later stages of healing.

Anger & Panic:
For those stuck in the Disillusionment and/or Treatment stages, overwhelming frustration with lack of healing improvement can bring up combinations of anger, rage and panic in chronic Lyme patients.

Depending on the patient, they can react either *externally* or *internally* and this can have a bearing on whether the patient experiences anger or panic. Patients who react *externally* are more prone to anger and tend to get frustrated with their family members, doctors and support systems. They can flare into rages that alienate them from the very people trying to help them. Further, they can feel unheard or marginalized when they complain of symptoms and don't receive validation from others. Because these patients tend to suffer from central nervous system irritation brought on by Bartonella and other co-infections, the term "Bartonella Rage" has become well-known in chronic Lyme communities.

If a patient reacts *internally*, they may be prone to fits of panic. It is common for Lyme patients to run out of money and support during the treatment stage, and these stressors can result in the patient feeling hopeless. When the bottom falls out of a patient's world like this and they have no energy to continue fighting the illness, suicidal thoughts occur. It is an unfortunate fact that suicide continues to be the leading cause of death in Lyme patients in the United States.

For these reasons, it is important for patients to move beyond this stage. Furthermore, the anger and panic they experience actually worsens symptoms and helps the bacteria and co-infections thrive. Those who have come to terms with their anger and panic find they have more energy reserves to heal. They place their focus on moving on with their lives vs. feeling the need to prove the injustices they have experienced. To be sure, they have suffered real injustices, but it is exhausting and energy draining to spend your time proving yourself to an unsympathetic audience. Placing focus on happier thoughts, successes and positive pursuits has always proven to be a powerful component to healing, and it is the key to helping patients move on from this stage.

Acceptance:

A patient who has accepted his/her situation is one who is ripe for healing. It doesn't mean they have resigned themselves to failure. It means they have stopped resisting, and by doing so have stopped the energy cycle of opposing force from the disease. Many alternative healers will tell you the less energy and attention you give to an illness, the less resistance you will get back from it. I noticed this during my own healing journey.

The more I focused on the symptoms and bad feelings the disease was causing, the worse I felt. Yet, there were times when I would watch a funny show on TV or listen to some music that made me forget I was sick. The more I strung those situations together into longer periods of time, the better and better I felt. Another way to let go of resistance during this stage is to stop identifying with the illness. Stop calling it "my disease" or "my symptoms." The bottom line and the best way to move through this stage is to accept the illness while also stopping the amount of energy and attention you give it. Once negative focus on the illness has dwindled to almost nothing is when patients tend to move to the next stage.

Gratitude:

If the idea of being grateful for chronic Lyme disease coming into your life sounds ridiculous or unthinkable, you may not be ready for this stage. Those who have reached recovery openly accept this concept. In fact, it allows them to put the illness completely behind them and understand why it was introduced in their life in the first place. It helps to think of the disease as simply new information being introduced into one's life.

The illness is a doorway or fork in the road that can either take you upwards or downwards. Instead of reacting negatively, you can accept it gracefully and realize what a gift of experience you have been given. This experience can be like a forest fire that burns away all unnecessary elements in your life, while creating space for new growth. Yes, it burns things you deem valuable, but after those things are gone, you realize they weren't as important as you thought.

Further, you are forced into new situations and places in your life that can be better places than where you were before. Understanding this, I came to a point that whenever I felt a symptom occur, I lovingly embraced it, thanked it for the information, and then asked for it to go with love. Each symptom passed quickly after doing this. The patients who move through this stage always experience some sort of spiritual shift, and this shift usually results in them wanting to help others with the disease. In fact, there is not a single person I'm aware of who has reached full recovery without some kind of spiritual breakthrough involving their forgiveness of others and themselves for past injustices. Complete healing works on all three levels of you... mind, body and spirit. And if you only focus on one aspect of yourself, you will get the corresponding results. People who experience complete healing are all positive, open-minded, full of gratitude and free of regrets. They are emotionally "debt-free" and actively give thanks for the illness and the knowledge and experience it has given them.

* * * *

Later that summer, I started a local business called the Lyme Recovery Clinic & Detox Center. After helping patients all over the country through the Ticked Off Foundation, Nutramedix, a company that makes the Cowden protocol for Lyme patients, reached out to me to offer a discount for any patient who qualified for financial assistance through us. They also insisted that I get trained by Dr. Cowden himself. After I resisted several times, I agreed to drive to Harrisburg, PA and get the training. I felt a little strange being in a room with 15 doctors and myself, but I quickly absorbed the information, and the training enabled me to better help the patients I was already counseling. After a while, several of them told me that they were discontinuing visits to their doctors because they were too expensive and the help I was giving them was actually making them feel better. It didn't take me long to consider doing this in my local area, and after a chain of coincidences over the course of a few months, I soon had an office space, a website and a handful of local patients.

CHAPTER 29:
MAKING SENSE OF IT ALL

By the winter of 2017 I was feeling spiritually and energetically restless again. I was noticing energetic shifts in the Earth itself and witnessing many emotional and spiritual changes among my friends. I was feeling positive about adjustments I had made in my life for the better and was taking stock in the fact that a mere 10 years before I was very ill. I worked a corporate job that stressed me out, I was not eating well, and I was generally living life on the treadmill in the rat race of life. Now I was helping people on a daily basis. I had started two organizations to help Lyme patients, and in the summer of 2017, I started the Lyme Recovery Clinic in Darien, CT to help Lyme patients with non-pharmaceutical treatments in person.

But I still had some questions and nagging thoughts. Why am I here in this lifetime and what is my mission? And who was I in a past lifetime that might help me make sense of who I am now? Why did I feel such a connection with Yeshua (Jesus) and the Holy family?

I didn't know what to do about answering these questions, but as the thoughts persisted, a solution presented itself.

A friend of mine from a Facebook group I was a part of reached out to me one afternoon and asked if I'd be interested in doing a trade with her. She was interested in my skills as a remote energy healer as well as a web designer and she offered me a free past-life regression healing in return for some of my services. This was exactly what I was looking for.

We set aside a date and time and began the session over the phone. She walked me through some questions and statements that helped me achieve a relaxed state, and we set the intention and focus of the session on only accessing my past lives that had a direct bearing on my current one. This would more clearly reveal my mission and purpose for taking a life at this time.

German Monk

It took some time for me to get focused but when my friend asked me to look down at my feet (with my eyes closed), I began seeing sandals on them. When I looked around the scene in my mind's eye, I could see I was in a medieval town. I was wearing a monk's robe and it was apparent that that's what I was. I made my way home to the monastery and I realized I was in Germany in the 1300s.

My friend asked me to participate in a meal and asked me what I saw. The other monks and I were all eating very well, and our meal consisted of bread, cheese and beer that had all been made there at the monastery. She then asked me what particular role I played there, and the words, "I'm a scribe" blurted out of my mouth. I envisioned a scene where I was sitting at a type of raised writing desk that was in a kind of corridor, lined with windows. A few of us were copying older manuscripts and holy scriptures that were in bad repair. I was going beyond copying them. I was adding artistic flourishes and illustrations in the margins and taking great pains to make them look beautiful. I had a real sense of accomplishment and fulfillment from this work, and I really seemed to enjoy it. I suddenly got the impression that one of my elders was also handing me secret documents, scrolls and information under the table that was deemed "forbidden" because its content directly contradicted Church doctrine. I realized we could be killed simply by possessing this information, but I felt it needed to be saved and passed on to future generations.

My friend asked me to move onto the next significant event in this lifetime and I saw myself being ordained as a bishop. I was wearing red and white gowns and a large hat, but not long after this scene the words came out of me that, "we've been caught."

My friend asked me what happened next and I realized I'd been hanged for my offense of copying and hiding forbidden information. She asked me not to relive the unpleasant experience, and we asked for a healing so that I could transmute this negative energy into love and forgiveness.

Early American

Next, my friend asked me to move to another significant lifetime. I looked down at my feet and saw them wrapped in some sort of soft animal skins. I could see that I was standing in the American plains. I realized that this was Montana in the 1500s. I was a Native American brave, living in a teepee with my wife and infant child. We had no horses as a tribe, and we led a life of balance with nature.

My friend asked me the next significant event in this lifetime and I saw myself involved in building a large ceremonial building with long logs and spars that were lashed together with leather straps. We had no knowledge of nails, screws or other fasteners. I was not any kind of leader in this tribe. I was just simply a citizen, and I had an overwhelming feeling of satisfaction and beauty that this type of life was perfect. Everything about it was enjoyable.

My friend reflected that the reason this life came through was to show that this kind of living was possible, and it was possible to experience this type of beauty and love for an entire lifetime.

European Dandy

The next lifetime we investigated began in the same way as the others. My friend asked me to look down at my feet and I blurted out, "I'm wearing pilgrim shoes."

"Oh, so you're a pilgrim so you're in the United States?" she asked.

"No," I said. "They're LIKE pilgrim shoes. They're square-toed but they have no buckle." She then asked me to move up my legs and I saw white leggings and velvet knee breeches. I was also wearing a velvet vest and a large, fancy hat.

"I have a lot of money," I said. "I'm wealthy and it feels good. I don't have to work. All of my money comes from my family. I lead a pretty easy life. I'm living somewhere in Western Europe in the 1700s."

My friend asked me to move to the next significant event in this life and I saw myself in the back of my covered carriage being robbed at knifepoint by two men. My driver was killed on the spot and I was stabbed in the lower abdomen. I didn't die from those wounds directly, but I did pass several days later from an infection caused by the wounds.

I mentioned out loud that the stab wounds correlate to two incisions made during an operation I had a year ago to repair a hernia and to remove a fatty lipoma. My friend said that the infection related to me contracting Lyme disease, and we needed to heal the fact that I was subconsciously associating being punished for being wealthy with the attack and ensuing infection. We called in ascended masters to help with that healing process.

Child in Paris

As we moved onto the next lifetime, I quickly recognized it to be the life I had experienced in a meditation back in 2010 which is mentioned in Chapter 14. I re-experienced pieces of my life during the Paris flood of 1910, including the interaction with my mother who did not spare the rod on me. The new information I got was that she had committed suicide and had not died of an accidental drowning. She was a depressed person. She couldn't swim, and she simply threw herself into the River Seine, took a deep breath and died.

As mentioned before, I forgave her for her tough treatment of me and that had prompted her to take a new life in this lifetime. My friend and I made sure there were no lingering karmic issues to be dealt with, and we asked for healing and balancing to span through the ages.

Philip the Apostle

The final lifetime transpired at the end of the session out of chronological sequence when my friend asked if there was another past life that needed to be examined.

I saw myself in colorful robes, standing outside a temple or government building in Jerusalem in the time shortly after Jesus had been crucified. Everyone associated with him was being tracked down, questioned and then usually tortured and put to death. I was very close with him, and I needed confidantes to help me escape harm. I had found help from either a rabbi or government official who told me he had an idea and to meet him at this building.

Not long after waiting, I was captured by Roman guards and the sinking feeling of betrayal washed over me. The next thing I saw was me being crucified on a cross, overlooking a hillside with beautiful cypress trees.

My friend asked what my connection was with Jesus. I said, "I am his brother." And she asked which brother. I couldn't answer. I didn't know the name, and then suddenly it all flooded in. My name was Philip. I was Philip the Apostle and I was not the physical brother of Jesus. I was his "soul brother." I had come in a soul cluster when he had incarnated, and we were very close. The feeling of everything he and I had been through washed over me, and it made me very sad and I sobbed uncontrollably. It was heartbreaking, and it felt like I had been holding onto this for ages.

It took me days to integrate this information and energy, but it had a profound effect on my mood and thinking of who I am in this lifetime and what I'm here to accomplish.

CHAPTER 30:
THE GRATITUDE CURVE

As mentioned earlier in the book, it felt like Lyme disease was a forest fire that burned my life to the ground. Once I stopped fighting the fire and let it burn away the things I had once thought valuable, I began to learn from it and accept where I was. The empty spaces gave me room for new growth and my life moved in a different direction.

I imagined an imaginary Gratitude Curve. Depending on where I was on the curve, (in relation to my life, illness, etc.) it dictated the smoothness of the ride. The more gratitude I had, the easier things got. When I actively practiced gratitude, things got magical.

While fighting against illness was one step above victimhood for me, I saw how I could get stuck in that mentality and energy. Arguing with doctors and family members about medical treatment and endlessly seeking validation and understanding from them for what I was going through became exhausting. I realized that proving them wrong or triumphantly proving myself right to them would not happen easily and it was very draining. It would also be a hollow victory. So what if I proved myself right? Would it improve my health?

Once I stopped resisting and fighting, I had to face the monster head on. It was like running from a nightmarish creature in a dream, where you stumble, and the monster catches up to you. Instead of cowering in fear when it approached, I looked at what it had to teach me.

I realized I was going through this thing to help others. My life would take on a completely different trajectory now and it would be more purpose-driven. It wouldn't be about myself but about me helping others. And the others I would help would have the same epiphany to aid others when they healed. It would start a chain reaction of help and support for the stricken.

I had an overwhelming feeling of gratitude when I realized this, and I began forgiving anyone who I felt had wronged me along the way. I went one step further and stopped beating myself up for the horrible way I might have reacted in some of these situations, and by forgiving myself, it unlocked decades of trapped energy. It also wasn't just a mental process. I genuinely forgave everyone from my heart and felt very sorry for the struggles each oppressor had gone through to make them act so horribly towards me. I felt an emotional and even spiritual shift upon doing this.

All of this might seem counterintuitive, but the results were unmistakable. Forgiving someone who has wronged you unlocks a large amount of energy that allows *chi* (life force) to flow through your body for complete healing. The other component to this was I had to do this work internally and on my own. No one could really help me, and I couldn't go to a doctor or get a prescription for this to help heal me. There is no substitute for facing these uncomfortable thoughts and energies head on instead of trying to avoid them.

I also came to realize that the so-called "cure" that I was looking for manifested in a way that I had not imagined. It didn't come in pill form or some silver-bullet treatment. It was a combination of treatments, visits to John of God, and life-style changes that brought me to this point. In order to stay in complete recovery, I needed to maintain a way of life that focused on my improved health. I could never go back to the way I was doing things before because that would cause a relapse in every way. It took me a long time to realize the disease had manifested to point me away from those life choices, eating habits and self-destructive pursuits.

To maintain my best health, I realized I needed to look at the entire picture, not just my physical symptoms. I needed to give daily attention to my mind, body and spirit. The point was — after progressing from focus on the body, then the mind, then the spirit — to come back and look at how they all integrate. A wounded spirit (from abuse or trauma) will cause shockwaves in the mind. It causes daily release of stress hormones because of dis-empowering and angry thoughts. This trapped energy causes negative effects on the body, lowers the immune system and lets invading bacteria run wild. Conversely, a healed spirit allows the free flow of thoughts and energy. Negative thoughts are never trapped. They move through the spirit and mind and are processed in a way that doesn't harbor resentment or even the justification for your angry actions. You can't move on if you have the internal thought, "Well, it was certainly understandable for me to be pissed off because of that person's actions." You won't progress until you can look past your ego-driven reaction and look at the picture from a dis-entangled perspective. They say, "it takes two to tango," and once you realize that each of these dances is an opportunity for growth, you will stop looking at it from how they affected your personal feelings. These thoughts are not to be avoided, but they are transmuted from the negative into the positive. Gratitude and forgiveness are the antidote. Once they have been unlocked, the mind is open, and the body is free to heal itself.

To remain in a steady state of health, grace and peace I began doing most of these things on a daily basis (as regularly as I could):

1. Do one thing for myself, one thing for a stranger and one thing for my family. These positive actions don't have to be limited to one thing, but it is best to pay attention to all three recipients every day.
2. A daily meditation practice. To quote a famous Zen saying, "Meditate every day for 20 minutes, unless you don't have time. Then meditate for an hour."
3. A daily yoga breathing and posture practice. I do a form of Kriya & Hatha yoga that a friend taught me that I practice for about half an hour every day.
4. Earthing and sungazing. Every day when it's sunny, I try to go outside in my bare feet (yes, even when there's snow), connect with the earth and stare into the sun for 15 seconds per eye 45 minutes after dawn or 45 minutes before sunset. Do research about sungazing before trying this yourself.
5. Working out with heavy weights 1-2 times per week
6. Doing a 2-3 day water fast every six months or so to reset my immune system and digestive tract
7. Eating an organic diet that's free of gluten, dairy, sugar, alcohol, soy and corn.
8. Daily cold shower for 2-3 minutes while doing intense breathwork.

9. Daily intermittent fasting, i.e. going 15-18 hours without food to balance the digestive tract and immune system.

It's been more than 10 years since the day I sat down to chronicle this journey and story. As I mentioned in the earlier writing, I didn't know if it would have a happy ending or not. Well, the ending turned out a lot different than expected. I've come a long way from the state I was in to the place I now stand. I'm sharing this story in the hopes that it will help others move through their struggles with chronic disease to a better place — and possibly to a place where they feel compelled to help others.

RESOURCES:

The following websites are helpful resources to those seeking answers to chronic illness — especially Lyme disease and tick-borne illnesses:

- **www.abraham-hicks.com**: This is the original source material for the current *Law of Attraction* wave that is sweeping the world.
- **www.heathercumming.com:** Heather Cumming is a well-known tour leader, translator and interpreter serving John of God's mission.
- **www.lightrivermedia.com:** International speaker, teacher, author, and channel, Catherine Ann Clemett has been a healer and intuitive for nearly 40 years.
- **www.LymeKnowledge.com:** An easy-to-understand web resource written by Lyme patients to help broadcast the most accurate and up-to-date information on Lyme prevention, symptoms, diagnosis & treatments.
- **www.LymeRecoveryClinic.com:** a clinic launched in 2017 to help those suffering from Lyme disease and other chronic illnesses heal through all-natural, herbal supplements, intensive detox measures, and energy healing & counseling practices.
- **www.TickedOffFoundation.org:** A 501(c)3 non-profit organization whose mission is to provide financial assistance and support to Lyme disease patients over the age of 26 who are in crisis. The organization does this through grants and counseling in an effort to stem the tide of Lyme-related suicides.
- **www.TickedOffMusicFest.com:** The only ongoing music series solely focused on Lyme disease education, awareness and fundraising. It tends to go to areas where the rate of infection is high but awareness is low.
- **www.tomkenyon.com:** Tom Kenyon's work in brain/mind re-education is a scientifically-based art form that transforms consciousness in rapid and elegant ways.
- **www.wendyrosewilliams.com:** Wendy Rose Williams is a hypnotherapist specializing in past-life regression, a Reiki master energy healer, certified spiritual teacher and ordained minister.

Made in the USA
Middletown, DE
30 April 2021